I Didn't Kn[...] Could [...]

Worry-Free Strategies to Thrive in Retirement

Written By: **Mark J. Orr, CFP® RICP®**

Certified Financial Planner™
Retirement Income Certified Professional®

Will You OUTLIVE Your MONEY? Check this out!
Find Out in 9 Quick Steps
www.smartfinancialplanning.com/find-out-here/

Author of:
Retirement Income Planning: The Baby-Boomer's 2023
Guide to Maximize Your Income and Make it Last
Social Security Income Planning: 2024 Baby-Boomer's Guide
Get Me to ZERO: 7 Tax Strategies for a TAX-FREE Retirement

2nd Edition -- Copyright 2024

Reviews are important. This book was so new that it didn't have many reviews yet. So, I thought that I'd provide you with some screenshots of some of my other books on Amazon as of October 2022.

Social Security Income Planning: Baby Boomer's 2023 Guide to Maximize Your Retirement Benefits Kindle Edition
by Mark J. Orr CFP (Author) | Format: Kindle Edition
★★★★☆ ~ 292 ratings

See all formats and editions

Kindle	Paperback
$0.00 Kindle unlimited	$6.53 - $6.99
Read with Kindle Unlimited to also enjoy access to over 3 million more titles	You Earn: 14 pts ✓prime
$2.99 to buy	33 Used from $1.49
	7 New from $6.99

TAX-FREE Millionaire : How TRIPLE ZERO™ Plans Can Transform Your Future Retirement Kindle Edition
by Mark J. Orr CFP (Author) | Format: Kindle Edition
★★★★☆ ~ 99 ratings

See all formats and editions

Kindle	Paperback
$0.00 Kindle unlimited	$5.99
Read with Kindle Unlimited to also enjoy access to over 3 million more titles	You Earn: 12 pts ✓prime
$2.99 to buy	1 New from $5.99
You Earn 15 pts	

Kindle Rewards Beta

Get Me to ZERO™: Use the 2023 I.R.S. Tax Code to Pay as Little as ZERO Income Taxes During Retirement and Have a Better Life Kindle Edition
by Mark J. Orr CFP (Author) | Format: Kindle Edition
★★★★☆ 195 ratings

See all formats and editions

Kindle	Paperback
$0.00 Kindle unlimited	$0.00
Read with Kindle Unlimited to also enjoy access to over 3 million more titles	You Earn: 10 pts ✓prime
	5 Used from $1.51
	7 New from $3.51

Retirement Income Planning: The Baby-Boomers 2022 Guide to Maximize Your Income and Make it Last Paperback – July 27, 2016
by Mark J. Orr CFP (Author)
★★★★☆ ~ 90 ratings

Why I Wrote This Book and Who Should Read It

I am unapologetic in my reason for writing this book. It is very simple. I want to actually <u>educate</u> readers on how some annuities can help their retirement goals and how, when used properly, they can truly transform almost any decades-long period of being happily "unemployed."

As a CFP® and comprehensive retirement income planner, I am not one of those dinner-seminar annuity hawkers. There is no hype, as readers will discover in these pages. I will only ever mention/recommend any annuity when one clearly fits a client's stated goals and circumstances.

My WHY: To help people proactively maximize every one of their financial resources and opportunities so they can enjoy a much fuller life and make a positive impact on our world. Annuities, when appropriate, can play a role.

My HOW: I use a holistic, process-based planning approach that employs multiple advanced planning strategies to help my clients become more financially confident and secure today while preparing for a much more predictable, stress-free, and safer retirement.

My WHATS:
#1) I use multiple financial strategies/financial products to take as many risks (inflation risk, market risk, longevity and LTC risk, etc.) out of my clients' retirement as possible.
#2) I combine 7 synergistic tax strategies to help my clients get their future cash flow off the IRS's radar screen and legally pay as little income taxes as possible during their retirement. The earlier one gets started, the better.

As a financial fiduciary, my two main mantras are:

1) Don't Take Any More RISK Than Necessary to Reach Your Goals
2) Don't Pay Any More TAXES Over Your Lifetime Than You Are Legally Required to by the IRS

My whole financial planning practice boils down to two simple words: PROACTIVE Planning. Planning for good and bad markets, tax increases, needing LTC, rampant inflation, and the granddaddy of them all—living too long.

The people who should read this book come from many backgrounds and stages in their life. Many simply don't want to take stock market (or bond) risks with 100% of their life savings. How much risk are you willing to take?

Others hate paying income taxes on interest that they are not even spending—adding to their annual tax burden.

Believe it or not, many folks, for whatever reason, haven't saved enough money to retire as "well" as they had hoped for. Or they want to enjoy a lifestyle that their savings may not be able to support for 20-35+ years with conventional portfolios and planning. They, too, need to read this book.

My promise to you is after reading the book, you will have learned at least 3 new and meaningful financial truths and/or different planning ideas—or I have dispelled more than one common falsehood you hold about annuities.

Visit **SmartFinancialPlaning.com** and check out my BLOG, etc., for many more interesting topics and planning ideas.

What's Inside This Book

Why I Wrote This Book and Who Should Read It   Pg. 3

Annuities? Are You Kidding Me?   Pg. 6

Does the 4% Rule Work?   Pg. 15

What's Sequence of Returns Risk?   Pg. 19

How Indexed Annuities Work   Pg. 33

Accumulation Annuities   Pg. 42

Bonds Vs. Buffer Annuities   Pg. 49

My RMD and Withdrawal Strategy   Pg. 69

FIAs That Offer Guaranteed Lifetime Income   Pg. 81

Special Situation FIAs Worth Knowing About   Pg. 105

An Interesting Life Insurance Alternative for IRAs   Pg. 110

A True Long-Term Care (LTC) Annuity   Pg. 114

Taxes and the Death of a Spouse in Retirement   Pg. 115

Ruling From the Grave—Stretching an Inheritance   Pg. 118

Vanguard's 10-Year Market Predictions   Pg. 120

The Two Retirement Doors   Pg. 122

About the Author and Much More   Pg. 131

Annuities? Are You Kidding Me?

Let's start by dealing with the elephant in the room.

You've probably seen the TV and magazine ads from the guy who "hates annuities... and thinks you should too." He owns one of the biggest investment advisory firms in the country and is worth $6.3 BILLION (Forbes Richest 400 List—#150 on 2022 list). Like me, he is a financial fiduciary.

His commercials say that he "would rather die and go to hell than sell an annuity" and "I'll never sell an annuity." He's mostly talking about very high-cost variable annuities sold by many stockbrokers. I wouldn't sell one of those now, either! Variable annuities give you all the market risk (and potential gains) plus very high expenses.

I'm told that he spends $50 million/year on his TV, radio, print, and internet advertisements to lure new clients. Why does any firm need to spend millions to get clients?

He and his multi-millionaire clients don't need annuity income to pay their monthly expenses or keep their retirement savings safe. He could lose 95% of all of his assets in the stock market and still be very wealthy.

With his wealth, he doesn't have any longevity risk either. He could live to be age 650 and never run out of money. His financial position is very different from mine and yours. Wouldn't you say so? I wrote this book for you—not him!

There is one other reason why he hates annuities. He is not insurance licensed and doesn't get paid for them. His fee-only firm charges his clients a fee based on the amount of money his firm manages for the client. It's a fee for the "assets under management" (AUM) arrangement.

In fact, he makes so much profit in quarterly fees, he'll even pay any surrender charges or early withdrawal penalties one may have in an annuity they own—if they move those funds to his investment firm. Hmmm... maybe this partly explains how he is a multi-billionaire!

There's nothing wrong with fees in and of themselves. In fact, I and tens of thousands of other investment advisor reps across the country charge fees for assets under management (AUM) as well. It's the fastest-growing way to be compensated in the financial world (as opposed to being paid trading commissions like in the old days).

Even the U.S. government prefers fees over commissions, despite fees being way more expensive for clients over time. The added value must exceed the fee though.

Our firm is one of the larger Registered Investment Advisory (RIA) firms in the country and we do an excellent job managing client portfolios. As an aside, one of the points that makes us different from the rest, is that we can use multiple investment strategies within a single account. I typically use 4-7 different strategies in client portfolios.

Anyway, since he is a fiduciary like I am and must put his

client's interests before his own, I have a lot of important questions for him, and you should have them too:

1) Where are you going to put your client's money that is protected from the stock market and bond risk and can still earn respectable returns?

2) In what investments are you going to tell your non-multimillionaire clients (minimum investment with him is $500,000 according to his TV, radio, and print ads) to place money that they cannot afford to lose?

3) What investments do you offer your clients to take the sequence of returns risk off the table?

4) Which of your investments totally eliminate bond interest rate risk and bond default risk?

Other than money market accounts, he doesn't have one! In my mind, an advisor cannot truly be a fiduciary and have 100% of the client's best interest at heart, if one advises every single person (through advertising) that all annuities have no place in any retirement portfolio.

In fact, the best academic research (more studies are added annually) clearly shows that this "blanket" statement is false. Many studies show that annuities can increase retirement success—not running out of money.

No product is perfect. Not annuities. Not mutual funds. Nor are ETFs, CDs, cash value life insurance, real estate, savings accounts, private equity funds, hedge funds, etc. I can find problems/holes in all of the above. Easily!

There are over 100+ insurance companies that are selling some 900 different annuity products. Those 900 annuities come in all shapes, sizes, and colors.

Some are awful, some are good, and a few dozen can be really worth looking at. Some are very expensive while others have no cost at all—just like a CD from a bank.

Some have a specific purpose and do well at serving that purpose. Others try to be financial "Swiss army knives" that do a lot of things for you, but none particularly well.

Each place to put or "store" your savings has advantages and disadvantages. Annuities are no different. When used properly, they can perform their job/role very well indeed as you'll learn in this book. And do so safely.

Fixed annuities (FAs) are very similar to 3, 5, or 7-year CDs. They generally pay a fixed interest rate that is higher than CDs for the whole period. Sometimes, there is a "bonus" on the first-year rate. These annuities are not usually very liquid until the end of the period, which is a negative. CDs also have penalties for early surrender, though.

But all annuities offer tax deferral, which "1099" CD accounts do not (you pay taxes on the interest annually). That's a positive along with the fact that the interest rates are usually higher with fixed annuities than CDs.

And the rates for new annuity contracts change (up or down) fairly often—just like new CD offerings at the bank.

But in this book, I'll focus on various special fixed <u>indexed</u> annuities (FIAs) that many agents don't know about, don't have access to, don't qualify to market them, or just don't know how to explain them to clients.

What you'll read in the pages that follow are some very specific cases where an annuity can do something very special and what no other product can do. And I bet that you will be saying, "I didn't know annuities could do that!" Hence, the title of this book.

I often say that financial products are only tools or "financial golf clubs." Each one performs its duty well, but not the role of the other tools or golf clubs. A hammer is meant to put a nail into wood. A saw can't do that, but it cuts wood very well. Pliers can't put a screw into something easily. That's what a screwdriver is for, right?

A putter isn't used on the tee (even for a short par 3), and a sand wedge can't reliably sink a putt from 5 feet away.

So, the role of fixed indexed annuities (FIAs) is to <u>safely</u> provide for either accumulation without market risk, a guaranteed lifetime income for one or both spouses, or as you'll see, some pretty cool specific financial roles.

But many wonder, "why they should give up the market's upside" in return for lower returns with more guarantees?

Well, in my mind, fixed-indexed annuities were never meant to compete with stocks or equity mutual funds, ETFs, private offerings, hedge funds, and the like. They are bond alternatives meant to balance out the volatility and risk of the stock market. Once you understand that concept, you will likely be more open to learning about indexed annuities and what they can do for you.

Now, obviously, annuities are not appropriate for everyone. And most good advisors will only recommend the right/best annuity to fix the problem/concern at hand.

Certainly, you shouldn't have more than 70% or so invested in them. You may not even want 20% of your savings in an annuity(s). Maybe no money at all if you don't want or need any "safe money" besides CDs.

And that's all right. I'm OK with that. As a fiduciary, based on a client's concerns, worries, and financial situation, I may never even bring up the "A" word (annuity).

But I've found that most people need some additional guarantees that only annuities can provide with greater earning potential than savings accounts/CDs with the additional benefit of tax deferral for non-qualified money.

Having said that, most people should have some stock market exposure. Here's why. Although stocks have a greater risk of loss, they also have a greater potential for big gains. Look at all the years with gains from 10%-20% and gains 2-4 times as large in the last three columns.

-40% or less	-40% to -30%	-30% to -20%	-20% to -10%	-10% to 0%	0% to 10%	10% to 20%	20% to 30%	30% to 40%	40% or more
					1993				
					2004				
					1968				
					1926				
					2016				
					1959				
					1965				
					2014	1982			
					1960	1971	1999	1991	
				2000	1994	2010	2017	1950	
				1962	2015	2006	1983	2019	
				1932	2011	2012	1963	1985	
				1946	1970	1964	1996	1989	
				1929	2005	1988	1951	1980	
				1969	1947	2020	1967	1936	
				1977	2007	1952	1976	2013	
			1973	1981	1948	1949	1943	1955	
			1941	2018	1987	1986	2009	1997	1958
			2001	1990	1984	1979	1961	1945	1928
		1974	1940	1953	1978	1972	1998	1975	1935
	2008	1930	1957	1934	1956	1944	2003	1995	1933
1931	1937	2002	1966	1939	1992	1942	1938	1927	1954

PROACTIVE ✓
Tax Planning

Wade Pfau, Ph. D., CFA, is a Professor of Retirement Income in the Ph.D. program at the American College. He holds a doctorate in Economics from Princeton University and is very well respected in the discipline of retirement income. He is the co-editor of the Journal of Personal Finance and has published many articles in financial industry journals, as well as the Wall Street Journal, New York Times, Money Magazine, etc. He is also a large contributor to the RICP® designation curriculum. In his works, he writes about two fundamentally different retirement income philosophies he calls "probability-based" and "safety-first." Each one has its own pros and cons. Primarily choosing one belief over the other will set the overall direction and predictability of one's retirement lifestyle and future income.

Those favoring "probability-based" will rely on the belief that the markets will provide large enough returns over time to compensate for the occasional yet likely negative returns. They say, "Why should I give up the upside" in return for lower returns with more guarantees?

The "probability-based" folks say that over time, your returns will work out OK. They can rightfully say that stocks have returned about 10% a year over the last 100 or so years. But as anyone can plainly see above, those annual returns are all over the place – and very random.

However, opponents point out that this philosophy leaves folks with both market risk (sequence of returns discussed in a moment) and longevity risk (living too long). This might mean outliving one's money and cutting lifestyle.

The "safety-first" mindset believes that <u>at least the essential costs of living expenses</u> should be covered by guaranteed income from Social Security, pensions, and fixed income annuities. These income sources are guaranteed and eliminate both sequence of returns risk and the risk of living too long and outliving your money.

Lifestyle expenses "over" your monthly necessities and leaving a future legacy could be met by using market-based investments. They believe this is more prudent. The "safety-first" folks feel that this philosophy reduces both stock and bond risk (sequence of returns discussed later) and longevity risk. These risks might mean outliving one's money and having to cut lifestyle.

Although this book primarily teaches how to take some stock and bond risk off your table—that S&P 500 bell curve chart above shows that most will already be taking plenty of risk with the equities in their portfolio.

Again, the "safety-first" mindset believes that at least the essential costs of living expenses should be covered by guaranteed income from Social Security, pensions, and fixed-income annuities. These income sources are guaranteed and reduce stress and the risk of living too long and thereby outliving your money.

Lifestyle expenses "above" your monthly necessities and leaving a legacy could be met by using market-based investments. They believe this is more prudent.

That "safety-first" thinking is what many of my retirement income planning clients want to be incorporated into their own income plans. Does that sound like you?

Do you remember the "what's your number" commercials on TV? You know, the ones that had people carrying around big orange numbers that represented the amount they would need to retire.

Their retirement savings goal. What number did you think was "your number?"

Do you have any idea where to start setting your number goal? Was it $350,000? $1,000,000? $2,500,000? My retirement income planning shows what your number is based on the assumptions we want to use. But I digress...

Anyway, maybe you saw an article in Money Magazine years ago that talked about the "4% rule" as it relates to your "number." Here's what it is (or was) all about.

Does the 4% Rule Work?

Maybe you saw an article in Money Magazine or elsewhere years ago that talked about the "4% rule." It's Suze Orman's and many other so-called sages "rule of thumb" for retirement income planning.

Here's what it is (or was) all about. In 1994, financial planner William Bengen developed the 4% rule. It quickly became the guiding "formula" used by professional advisors and do-it-yourselfers for about two decades.

The 4% rule (or theory) says that at retirement, with a portfolio of 60% stocks and 40% bonds, one could withdraw 4% of the initial savings (and increase it by inflation every year). Then, the retiree would have a 90% chance of his income continuing for 30 years without the savings being completely depleted until the end of those 30 years.

By the way, a 100% stock or a 100% bond portfolio has less than a 60% chance of lasting 30 years. A portfolio of

100% CDs doesn't have a prayer. The research shows that under most long-term market scenarios (backcasting), a 60%/40% portfolio worked the best.

So, for example, someone with $1,000,000 at retirement could withdraw $40,000 in the first year. If inflation was 3% that year, the 2nd year, they could withdraw $41,200. That growing income could conceivably last for 30 years until the savings and income stream would be all gone.

Of course, it's even possible that your account could be much larger at the end of 30 years. Or it may not last 30 years at all. The 4% rule (and similar rules) fall under Dr. Wade Pfau's "probability-based" income philosophy rather than the "safety-first" approach.

Have you already decided which mindset you favor? If you got on a plane and the pilot announced the "good news" is that there is a 90% chance of landing safely at your destination, would you get off that plane? I would!

The stock markets were at all-time highs at the end of 2021... until they weren't. And then the end of the 30-year-long bull market in bonds has come with rising interest rates. Now inflation is at 40-year highs. Do you believe a 90% chance is optimistic now? Who knows?

Mr. Bengen understands that as interest rates rise, the value of bonds will drop. This makes a diversified portfolio of even 30%-40% bonds riskier now. The other reason this theory is not blindly used nearly as much anymore is largely due to something called the "sequence of returns" risk.

I'll be writing more about this investment risk in the pages that follow. In broad terms, the sequence of returns risk is that stock losses early in your retirement can have a major effect on whether you outlive your money or not.

But for now, I'll leave it at that. Morningstar has recently upped its "safe" withdrawal rate from 3.3% in 2021, 3.8% in 2022, and now back up to 4% based on the higher yields in bonds today.

That means that a $1,000,000 retiree could withdraw $40,000 in their first year of retirement and have that figure grow by inflation each year. Does $40,000/year on $1,000,000 sound impressive to you?

What if you/your spouse need income for more than 30 years? It does happen and will happen more often.

A Wall Street Journal article once stated: "If you had retired Jan. 1, 2000, with an initial 4% withdrawal rate and a portfolio of 55% stocks and 45% bonds rebalanced each month, with the first year's withdrawal amount increased by 3% a year for inflation, your portfolio would have fallen by a third through 2010, according to investment firm T. Rowe Price Group. And you would be left with only a 29% chance of making it through three decades, the firm estimates."

The last sentence is the real potential warning. Again, my next question, is what if you (or your spouse) live longer than 30 years in retirement? We are retiring earlier and living longer! It's a strong possibility for many folks as longevity is by far the largest of the risks in retirement. These "rules" ignore an income need over a longer potential retirement for you and/or your spouse.

The 4% rule also ignores the huge financial implication of a spouse needing long-term care (LTC) or some other major expense on the balance of the 30-year retirement.

Now, many folks believe there is no way that they will live 30 years in retirement. But I'll remind you that if a couple has made it to age 65, there is a 50% probability that at least one of them will live to age 92 and a 25% chance at least one of them will celebrate their 95th birthday (and perhaps more). Those statistics are actuarial facts.

And for better-educated, wealthier, and healthier retirees, the odds of living longer than that are even better. The strides being made every year in medical science are well-known. Cancer could be cured, and heart attacks avoided. We can only hope.

In any case, would you rather plan on a 20-year retirement and be out of luck if you (or your spouse) live 25 years... or plan on a 35-year retirement income stream and only live 25 years? Unless your and/ or your spouse's health is not good, I hope that the answer is self-evident.

Many investors have a hard time understanding that if their portfolio earns 4%, and they take out 4% every year for living expenses, why would their principal go down? Shouldn't it stay level forever?

The problem with that logic is that it fails to take inflation into account. If your expenses are going up (compounding) by 2%-3% a year, then your portfolio would have to gain that much each year on top of the 4% you take out.

And over time, the bite of inflation is harsh. At just 3% inflation, your monthly expenses will double in about 24 years. Your portfolio would have to do the same despite withdrawals for your principal to stay level.

That logic also fails to account for the potential of rising taxes. If taxes go up, you'll need to withdraw more money out of your accounts just to live the same lifestyle.

OK, now let's add the biggest wrinkle to the 4% rule—the Sequence of Returns Risk.

What's Sequence of Returns Risk?

This is how the mutual fund company Thornburg Investment Management defines sequence of return risk: "Sequence of returns is simply the order in which returns are realized by a retiree. The consequences of a bad sequence of returns, especially early in retirement, can mean a premature depletion of the portfolio. Retirees need to avoid being in the position of having to sell during inopportune market environments."

I'll add more practical value and an eye-opening example in a moment.

Given the recent height of the market, it should be a warning. Rob Williams, managing director of income planning at the Schwab Center for Financial Research says: "When you're withdrawing funds at the same time that your portfolio is losing value, you can expose yourself to a phenomenon known as sequence-of-returns risk.

The sequence (order) in which investment returns occur can have a huge impact on your assets' long-term if you are taking withdrawals from (or even adding to) your portfolio."

The biggest risk is during the withdrawal phase. Let me be clear that the sequence of returns risk does not apply to a lump sum of assets and holding. Only spending.

The risk is only dangerous while taking an income stream from your savings—particularly when the investment returns early in your retirement are hugely negative or very poor.

You've heard the expression, "timing is everything." Well, your sequence of returns could work for you... or against you in taking income from your investments, as you'll see. Here's an example of how a poor sequence of returns can destroy a long-term retirement plan.

And just for "old-times-sake," I'll also use a 5% withdrawal rate (adjusted for inflation) in the example. So many people still think that if a portfolio averages 7%, then taking a 5% withdrawal rate should leave them with a larger balance than they started with 30 years from now!

That's not correct, as it ignores the compounding effect of inflation – which can be a powerful headwind against a successful retirement.

Let's look at the actual returns of the S&P 500 index (with no fees or taxes) from 1989 to 2008. Then, let's take those same exact returns and reverse the order they came in (2008-1989). You'll notice that both sequences have the exact same average return of 8.49% (a typo in the chart).

There is no difference in the average rate of return—if withdrawals are not being taken. The sequence of returns has no effect on a lump sum with no withdrawals.

The middle column is the actual price returns of the S&P 500 from 1989 to 2008. The column on the far right is the same exact index returns... but in reverse order (2008 back to 1989). The same index, just a different order of returns.

If we have a hypothetical account valued at $1,000,000, and we withdraw $50,000 (5%) and adjust that for inflation (we'll use a 3% constant inflation rate for all years), let's see how the two sequences of returns (the actual S&P 500 index returns plus the same returns in the reverse order) play out. (Avg. has a typo in the chart).

Year	1989-2008 Sequence	2008-1989 Sequence
1	31.69%	-37.00%
2	-3.11%	5.49%
3	30.47%	15.84%
4	7.62%	4.91%
5	10.08%	10.88%
6	1.32%	28.68%
7	37.58%	-22.10%
8	22.96%	-11.88%
9	33.36%	-9.11%
10	28.58%	21.04%
11	21.04%	28.58%
12	-9.11%	33.36%
13	-11.88%	22.96%
14	-22.10%	37.58%
15	28.68%	1.32%
16	10.88%	10.08%
17	4.91%	7.62%
18	15.84%	30.47%
19	5.49%	-3.11%
20	-37.00%	31.69%
AVG.	8.43%	8.49%

Withdrawals start at $50,000/ year and rise to $90,000 annually over the 2 decades (to combat inflation). After only 20 years of retirement, the 1989-2008 sequence has more than supported the retirement spending and even allowed the account value to grow to over $3.1 million. The early years of good returns made this possible. The big losses came in the 2nd half of the two decades. In this example, the "probability-based" model worked out perfectly. But that's a hope, not a plan.

Continuing to take out $90,000 plus 3% inflation withdrawals isn't going to pose a problem at all for that 30-plus year retirement. But this isn't a typical bull market. I certainly wouldn't want to plan my own retirement income stream on a possible 20-year bull market.

Again, "timing is everything." Timing and the "probability-based" model could work well for you and dramatically increase your saving—or against you in taking income from your investments, so you outlive your savings.

And the differences could be very dramatic, with wide swings in possible outcomes. However, the results for the 2008-1989 sequence (reverse order) are very different, with the heavy losses coming in the first half of the period.

The first-year loss of -37%, which was followed by significant negative returns (3 years in a row) in years 7, 8, and 9 dramatically reduced the total account value to only about $235,000 at the end of the 20 years.

With an account balance of just $235,000 at the end of 20 years, there is virtually no way that anyone could take out $90,000 a year at that point and last more than three years before the account would run dry.

In this case, the "probability-based" philosophy would not have worked out so well. In fact, it would have been a disastrous outcome for a 30-year retirement.

So, the sequence of returns while taking income withdrawals had a huge swing in potential outcomes.

I can also show you actual annual returns when the S&P 500 averaged 9% a year—with only a 4% withdrawal rate (the 4% rule) and the portfolio blew up. Out of money!

On the rosier side, the account could more than triple – despite taking substantial income along the way. On the opposite end of the spectrum, with a bad sequence of returns, the account could diminish by -73% and have no shot of providing even a 24-year income to the retiree.

The range of possible retirement income risks and outcomes is probably wider than it's ever been with the globalization of our economy. We could see high stock returns, big negative stock returns, high inflation, deflation, higher taxes, and more changes in government policy (Social Security, Medicare, etc.).

As you'll read in an upcoming chapter, the floor of a 0% return, fixed indexed annuities can help retirees lessen the pain of the sequence of returns risk and perhaps virtually eliminate this huge risk to your retirement savings —whether taking Required Minimum Distributions (RMDs) or just taking withdrawals to meet your living expenses.

Financial advisors David Gaylor and his partner Gary Reed are 2 of my friends and mentors as well. David writes a story in his book that we use in our educational classes, teaching retirement income planning to pre-retirees. I'm going to pass it along to my readers here – giving full credit where it's due!

It is the story of 2 sisters, Jane and Jill, who are three years apart in age. But all the other circumstances they share are identical. The only difference is, "Jill was born three years too late!"

You see, Jane retired with $1,000,000 in 1996, and Jill retired three years later in 1999. Jill had an equal amount of savings to her older sister in her retirement. Only the "sequence of returns risk" is shown here—no other potential risks are factored in.

Both had heard on the radio that they should only invest in low-cost index funds (to pay virtually no fees). They were both excited about the big returns in the US stock market. In the late 1990s, everyone was making money.

In fact, the index returns lagged most individual companies' returns in the tech sector, but they liked the idea of diversification at a low cost. Set it and forget it!

When Jane retired in 1996, she began using the 4% rule, which had really become popular in the 1990s and was talked about on the radio and in magazines as a "safe" way of not running out of money for 30 years.

So, Jane started taking an income of $40,000 and increased her withdrawals by a 3% constant inflation rate each year to keep her purchasing power equal to inflation.

Jane retired at an excellent time. She had very good returns in 1996, 1997, 1998, and 1999. Yes, she suffered like almost everyone else in 2000-2002.

But starting with those first 4 years, and even considering seven years of increasing withdrawals, her account never dipped below $1,000,000. And during the recovery of 2003-2007, her account actually grew to nearly $1.5 million—while continuing to take income that had grown to over $55,000 a year by then.

Despite her income growing to about $68,000 in 2014 and suffering through the 2007-2009 bear market (the worst since the Great Depression), her account was still worth nearly $1.5 million. Jane took out over $1,000,000 in withdrawals over those 19 years, and her account actually grew by +49% on top of that!

The sequence of returns happened to be "on her side." Of course, it was just luck. No skill or advanced planning. Jane ended up in great shape for the next 10, 15, or even 20 years. She will have no income worries and have real peace of mind. And she'll be able to leave a nice legacy for her children, grandkids, and/or charity. Relying on "probability-based" planning worked well in this case.

But the timing of her retirement was purely by chance!

Now let's look at what happened to her younger sister Jill. Retiring with the same $1,000,000—but her retirement picture would look very different only three years later. She used the same 4% rule as Jane and the same low-cost index funds. But the timing of her retirement was not very good.

As you'll see, the randomness of the sequence of returns was not on "her side" when she started taking income in January 1999—even though the index returned +8.91% that first year. She would have been better off with "safety-first" thinking. Losses in 2000, 2001, 2002, and then a whopping loss in 2008 ruined the long-term health of her retirement.

Those investment losses, along with her $40,000 and growing distributions, caused her account value to drop to just over $316,000—just ten years into her retirement! That's a -68% reduction from her initial one million dollars of savings. Even though 2008 was the last year that she suffered a loss, by continuing those growing withdrawals, her account was only valued at $283,000 by the end of 2014—just 16 years into her retirement!

With 2015 being a very "flat" year in the index, her withdrawal of about $64,000 in that year would have left her account valued at some $220,000.

She "might" have only four or five years left of income before her savings are all gone. Then what? Ask Jane to take care of her significant income shortfall?

Now Jane and Jill's story only focuses on the sequence of returns. No changes in tax rates, inflation, health care costs, or public policy. The longer one lives, the larger those other risks become.

About a dozen years ago, a "brand-name" insurance company started teaching both advisors and consumers about something they called the "Retirement Red Zone."

They defined the retirement red zone as the five years right before you retire and the first five years of being retired. They promoted it pretty heavily, and it makes perfect sense and is completely in line with the reality of the sequence of returns risk.

But as we saw with Jill, those first ten years killed her "dream" retirement income plan. I prefer to alter the "red zone" definition to cover 5 to 15 years before retirement and the first TEN years of "unemployment!"

Are you a football fan? If so, you've heard the TV commentators talk about the "red zone" as the area within 20 yards of the goal line. The offense may have driven the ball all the way down the field and gotten close to scoring a touchdown. But defenses get stronger in the red zone, as there is less field to defend. It's harder to score in the red zone.

The NFL even has a statistic called "red zone efficiency." It is the percentage of times an offense scores a TD when they make it to the red zone.

What does football have to do with retirement?

Well, think of moving the football down the field as accumulating retirement savings. Then you get to the retirement red zone—the most critical time in retirement.

It's the hardest part to navigate and successfully "score" (being Jane rather than Jill). And that huge insurance company was only referring to risks of investment returns during those years—making no mention of the other risks to retirement (described on page 31).

The "probability-based" folks focus on the 90% chance of retirement success, while those identifying with the "safety-first" philosophy focus more on the 10% chance of retirement failure—outliving your money. I believe in "safety-first" planning for your basic and essential expenses. Use "probability-based" (getting both market risks and the rewards) for fun spending and legacy with much less stress! Our firm does this very well.

Always keep in mind that if you lose -35%, you need +53.8% returns—just to get back to even.

And it's not only stocks that can lose money. Bonds can lose value too. Even bonds that the US government guarantees can lose money (if sold before maturity).

The Bloomberg Barclays U.S. Long-Term Treasury Total Return Index is currently (early 2022) experiencing its most significant drawdown (loss of value) to date.

Percent Loss	Percent Gain
5%	5.3%
10%	11.1%
15%	17.6%
20%	25.0%
25%	33.3%
30%	42.9%
35%	53.8%
40%	66.7%
45%	81.8%
50%	100.0%

It's plummeted more than 20% as Long-Term Treasuries continue to sell off amid skyrocketing inflation expectations, lifting the U.S. 10-year Treasury Yield to 1.75% from under .75% in 2021.

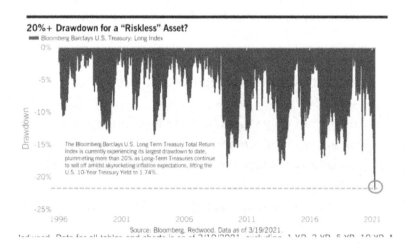

20%+ Drawdown for a "Riskless" Asset?

Bloomberg Barclays U.S. Treasury: Long Index

The Bloomberg Barclays U.S. Long Term Treasury Total Return Index is currently experiencing its largest drawdown to date, plummeting more than 20% as Long-Term Treasuries continue to sell off amidst skyrocketing inflation expectations, lifting the U.S. 10-Year Treasury Yield to 1.74%.

Source: Bloomberg, Redwood. Data as of 3/19/2021.

A 20% drop in value for what is thought to be the safest investment in the world! More clear and compelling evidence shows that bonds should not be as prevalent in portfolios right now, and bond alternatives such as annuities should be fully explored!

And you are in the right place to do so. What's the answer for somebody planning on retiring in the next 1-10 years? Or are you already in the first 1-10 years of retirement?

There are six major risks during retirement, and some annuities can help mitigate all of them to some degree.

Those risks are market risk, inflation risk, tax risk, a spouse dying too soon, long-term care (LTC) risk, and perhaps the biggest risk of them all—longevity risk.

We've just talked about market risk (sequence of returns) and inflation risk (at 3% inflation, you'll need twice as much income to enjoy the same lifestyle 24 years hence).

Tax rate risk is so under-planned for (assuming any real planning has been done at all. Not only do I believe tax rates will increase for almost all of us (except for the poor) due to our $34+ TRILLION of federal debt, but also, most folks don't understand what happens to their taxes when a spouse passes away. They go up!

A couple with taxable income (2024) of $23,200 has a marginal tax bracket of just 12%. All income above that (to $94,300) gets taxed at 22%!

But when a spouse passes, that marginal tax bracket gets cut in half the following year to only $47,150. But did the survivor's income get cut in half? Probably not!

And speaking of a spouse dying too soon, not only will their tax situation likely change for the worse, two Social Security checks will be reduced to keeping the largest check and losing the smaller one. And perhaps a pension might be cut in half or lost entirely depending on choices made at retirement. The death of a spouse and its effect on taxes and possibly even Medicare is discussed later.

And too few folks have done planning for the likely case that at least one of them may need LTC. The research shows that 2/3 of us will need care at some point. We all know that home care or assisted living and nursing home care are very expensive.

And finally, longevity risk. Why might that be the greatest risk of all? Well, the longer one lives, the greater the chances that one or all of the other five risks will occur.

Keeping in mind those six retirement risks, I run my retirement "safety-first" practice and design my client's written retirement income plans under the guidance of the four "S's": Smart, Secure, Simple, and Solutions.

Smart means that you don't take ANY more risks than you need to achieve your goals and don't OVERPAY taxes!

Is there really any potential return worth losing sleep over and putting much of your life savings at risk? Is it 11%, 16%, or 20%? How much risk are you willing to take? How much risk can you afford to take? How much risk do you want to take? And doesn't the IRS get enough already?

Secure means thinking more about your downside protection than a potential upside gain. Consider the "What IF you're wrong?" scenario for any number of life's unforeseen events (retirement risks).

Simple. People must understand their plan and why they are taking any particular step to improve their chances of success. It must be 100% transparent too.

And finally, **Solutions.** Retirement planning is much more about "planning" than "products." Products just fill the need. So, planning solutions (any financial products and services) must encompass the other three S's.

Do your retirement planning strategy and written income plan comply with the four S's at this point?

So those are the major risks to a successful retirement (not running out of money). Annuities (FIAs) can help mitigate those risks entirely (market risks, inflation risk, and living too long) or partially do so with the other 3 risks.

How Indexed Annuities Work

Let me briefly describe how most FIXED INDEXED ANNUITIES (FIAs) work and avoid stock market risk.

Once we've learned how FIAs work, you'll learn how I use the sub-categories of FIAs 1) special accumulation annuities that are part of my retirement income/Required Minimum Distributions (RMDs) strategy to improve on and make the 4% rule actually work and 2) attractive guaranteed lifetime income annuities—without losing access to your money!

Then, I'll show you what some "special situation" FIAs can do for your retirement that will likely surprise you. As I stated earlier in the book, not every insurance agent has access to these or even knows they exist. And perhaps more importantly, know how to position these unique products (tools) as part of an overall income plan.

As the name fixed indexed annuity implies, the interest "return" is determined by an index or indexes such as the S&P 500, Dow, or the Bloomberg Bond index.

Once you pay your annuity premium to the insurance company, the company invests those premium dollars into their general account, which is mostly invested in high-quality bonds that pay interest.

The insurer could pay you an interest rate like a CD from what it earns on its bond investments minus its overhead, expenses, and profit margin. Your bank does something very similar in that it pays the depositor an interest rate that depends on its loan portfolio interest income minus its overhead, expenses, and profit margin.

Many FIAs will offer their policyholders a one-year fixed rate of 2.5%-4.5% or so (fixed account) right now. Better than most banks have been before 2023, but not very appealing to most folks or, frankly, to me.

As the owner of an FIA, you have the right to forego getting that fixed interest rate and have those interest payments buy options on an index(es) such as the S&P 500, NASDAQ, etc.

By using options, you can participate in the upside of the index when it goes up. But there is a catch—you don't get all or even most of the "upside" in a good year. Why?

Because of the option strategy(s) you choose, you are "limited" in the amount of interest that can be credited to your annuity by a "cap," "spread," or a "participation" rate. I'll get to these terms in a moment.

Also, you can never get a loss by using options instead of investing your actual principal since your funds were never invested in the market. And the worst thing that can happen with the option strategies the insurer uses, is that the options expire worthless. When that happens, no interest is credited to your policy that year. In other words, you get a zero return.

When the indexes crash like in 2000, 2001, 2002, 2008 and in early 2022, ZERO is your hero! It's much better to get NO return—than to experience a big loss. Your principal can never go backward due to losses in an index.

With no losses, there is no sequence of return risk either.

And when the index goes up because of the use of options, your gain is limited by a cap, spread, or participation rate.

A "cap" is the <u>most</u> the interest will credit in one year (say 7%), based on the index used, the cost of the options, and the amount the insurance company can spend on the options (which are about equal to the interest they would have paid you in the fixed account).

A "participation rate" (par rate) means that you would get a certain percentage of the index's gain, such as 55%. A participation rate can give you the potential for more upside in a BIG year.

So, with a participation rate of 55%, if the index went up by 6%, your policy would be credited with an interest rate of 3.3% that year. When the index earns 11.2%, with a 55% par rate, your interest credit would be 6.105%. You never participate in any index losses, so zero is your hero.

Like participation rates, a "spread" also allows for some more potential gains when the index has big gains. With a "spread," the insurer uses that spread percentage to buy more options.

A 2.75% spread means that you don't get any interest credited unless the index beats that amount (the spread).

You get ALL the gains above that amount credited to your policy. For example, if the index does 7.75%, with a 2.75% spread, your account would be credited with 5% interest. If the index returned 11%, you would get credited 8.25%. If the index only did 2%, the spread is larger than the gain, and you would get no interest that year. You never have to endure a market-based loss.

Now, some FIAs (BUFFER annuities) give YOU the option every year to pay a little bit (an optional fee) so the insurance company can buy more options. With some other FIAs, that fee is part of the contract. You don't have a choice.

What does that do for you? It gives you more UPSIDE. With a fee (included or optional), you enjoy much higher PARTICIPATION rates, lower SPREADS, or higher CAPS!

There are two additional attractive features of all FIAs that you should know about. These features set them apart from almost every other type of investment. They are called the lock-in feature and the annual reset.

The "annual lock-in" feature says that once interest is credited to your account, it becomes principal, and at that point is never subject to future market losses.

Those gains become part of your protected account value. On every policy anniversary, any interest gained is credited to your account automatically and becomes principal. Past gains are never subject to future market losses.

The only way to lock in gains from hedge funds, stocks, bonds, mutual funds, real estate, etc., is to sell the asset. Of course, unless the asset is inside an IRA or similar IRS-qualified account, there will be a tax due on the gain.

In every annuity, there is no tax due until money is withdrawn. This is an important advantage if you are using investments from your taxable account (non-IRA funds) to purchase your FIA before retiring and not taking income yet.

You won't get a 1099 tax form or owe any tax until taking income out. Tax deferral is a powerful tool that allows you to control when you pay taxes and only on the amount of withdrawal. You'll see why later on.

The other nice feature is the "annual reset." This means that the beginning value(s) of the index or indexes you choose to allocate your funds into each policy year resets to the level where the indexes ended the previous year. This is a very valuable feature.

Here is an illustration of the lock-in and reset. The S&P 500 is the line that has big ups and downs. An FIA with only a 4% cap is the smoother ride. The lock-in feature ensures your principal never loses due to market losses.

These are real S&P 500 returns (without dividends) shown in this chart. The principal-protected FIA did pretty well against the uncapped index during that time period.

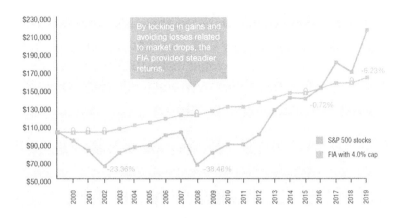

By locking in gains and avoiding losses related to market drops, the FIA provided steadier returns.

-6.23%

-0.72%

-23.36%   -38.48%

S&P 500 stocks
FIA with 4.0% cap

How is this important? Let's go back to October 16, 2007, and say you rolled over your 401(k) to buy a $400,000 FIA and had 100% of your index allocated to the S&P 500 index when the S&P 500 index closed at 1538 that day. A year later, on October 16, 2008 (your first policy anniversary), the S&P index closed at 946—a -38% loss.

As you know, because your principal was never invested in the market, your $400,000 did not lose a dime. Zero was your hero. This is where the annual reset comes into play.

For your next policy year, the index "resets" to where it ended the year before—at 946. Now, all of next year's interest that will be credited to your policy is calculated from that index value to where the index closes a year later—not from the original index price of 1538 when you bought the annuity.

On October 16, 2009, the S&P 500 index closed at 1087.

That is a 14.9% gain (subject to participation rates, caps, and/or spreads) and would be the basis of the interest credited to your policy that year. And now, for the next policy year, the reset would make 1087 the starting index value. This is very powerful—especially when accumulating retirement assets.

It doesn't work that way with stocks or mutual funds. If you retired and rolled over your 401(k) and bought $400,000 of the Vanguard S&P 500 mutual fund on October 16, 2007, there is no annual lock-in or an annual reset. Your mutual fund would have lost all -38% of what the index did in the first year you owned it. Your mutual fund would have lost a whopping $152,000.

And you would need a +61% gain in the index just to get you back to breakeven (from a -38% loss). Your principal is never protected with most investments, and your past gains are never locked in, either. FIAs protect your principal and past gains during a market crash and can perform pretty well during recovery periods.

In fact, five years after you bought that mutual fund, the S&P 500 index had still not reached the level where you initially invested (1538). On October 16, 2012, the index closed at 1455 (still well below that of Oct. 2007).

The annual lock-in and reset features can undoubtedly offset some of the disadvantages of not getting the full market gains in big up years due to the caps, spreads, and participation rates inherent in all fixed-indexed annuities.

All FIAs offer the potential for respectable gains when the index(es) do well but protect you from all losses and the sequence of returns risk when the markets go down.

In addition to many indexes available with caps, spreads, and participation rates, there are "time periods" that are used to measure potential returns and interest credited.

As just discussed, annual point-to-point calculates the index returns from the day your policy gets issued (your effective date) to a year later (your policy anniversary), and does so year after year. The index value at the start of the policy year is compared to one year later (subject to the caps, spreads, etc.).

Some policies only count index gains (lock-in and reset, too) every 2, 3, or even five years in order to determine your interest earned. There are also monthly averaging, monthly sum, and daily averaging indexing calculations. I'm sure there are or will be other methods as well that the insurers come up with over time.

Now that you have a better understanding of how fixed indexed annuities work in general, let's take a closer look at some of the past returns in accumulation annuities.

As stated earlier, in general, there are two main types of FIAs. One strictly for safely growing your savings and one to generate guaranteed lifetime income without annuitizing (giving up complete control of your asset immediately). Let's begin with the first type.

Accumulation Annuities

The main type of accumulation FIAs just offers principal-protected returns linked to an index, as previously discussed. There are generally no fees or any other benefits like guaranteed lifetime income (unless you annuitize, which I would very rarely recommend) or potential LTC-like benefits, etc. Just a safe place to grow your savings without market or sequence of returns risk on a tax-deferred basis.

The other type is what I refer to as a "BUFFER annuity." It is the same as above, BUT these FIAs give you the "option" to pay a fee in order to buy more options on the index(es) for much more upside. You can decide every year if you want to pay the fee for higher potential returns. In fact, I wrote a book about them.
When I wrote my book, -**BUFFER Annuities** - (my own name for them), there were only 2-3 of those products available. Now, there are many more to choose from.

And to muddy the waters a bit more, there are now accumulation FIAs that come with a fee (not optional) for built-in extra upside. That fee is used to buy more options. And some of these, despite the fees, are very attractive to my clients. Again, all financial products have pros and cons, just like everything else in this world.
The key is to know what you are trying to accomplish with the product (your goal) and then choose the annuity that

best delivers on that. Think household tools or golf clubs.

Let's start with an accumulation FIA illustration that has no fees, a deposit of $100,000, and no withdrawals shown.

This one has 6 indexes to choose from, and all are 2-year buckets. So, no interest is credited in years 1, 3, 5, etc. Only at the end of each two-year period. I chose 5 indexes for this illustration. These and all illustrations to follow assume the original allocation was never changed based on changing economic and market conditions.

All illustrations are based on index returns that have been backcasted, as these proprietary indexes did not exist 10-20 years ago. Proprietary indexes (not the S&P 500, DOW, or NASDAQ) are designed for higher potential returns at a lower option cost and are based on systematic rules-based computer algorithms.

There are no investment managers making human market and/or emotional predictions. The rules-based algorithms determine what to buy and sell and when to do so (based on what's happening in the markets, not why). The rules do not change based on market conditions since there is always a 0% floor to protect the principal.

With the 2-year indexes, interest is only credited at the end of each 2-year period. There are no fees, so there is less upside potential. I would feel comfortable planning for a 4%-6% average annual return over time with that product.

The Most Recent 10 index scenario reflects the performance of the annuity assuming the historical performance of the index over the most recent 10 calendar year period

Assumed Interest Rate	Accumulation Value
N/A	$100,000
23.81%	$123,811
N/A	$123,811
2.59%	$127,044
N/A	$127,044
19.98%	$152,650
N/A	$152,650
12.39%	$172,406
N/A	$172,406
9.65%	$190,008

Product Geometric Mean Interest Rate* = 6.63%

The Highest index scenario reflects the historical performance of the index for a continuous period of 10 years out of the last 20 years that would result in the most index value growth

Assumed Interest Rate	Accumulation Value
N/A	$100,000
35.99%	$135,990
N/A	$135,990
25.34%	$171,351
N/A	$171,351
10.23%	$189,117
N/A	$189,117
22.60%	$228,599
N/A	$228,599
20.71%	$275,927

Product Geometric Mean Interest Rate* = 10.68%

The Lowest index scenario reflects the historical performance of the index for a continuous period of 10 years out of the last 20 years that would result in the least index value growth

Assumed Interest Rate	Accumulation Value
N/A	$100,000
9.02%	$109,023
N/A	$109,023
8.94%	$118,454
N/A	$118,454
17.78%	$139,363
N/A	$139,363
11.74%	$155,171
N/A	$155,171
6.96%	$166,435

Product Geometric Mean Interest Rate* = 5.23%

The next chart (page 46) of a no-fee accumulation FIA has an 8-year surrender charge period and starts off with a $75,000 deposit. In this illustration, the client wanted to use 50% of the funds in 4 one-year indexes and the other 50% in the two-year indexes to determine how they are invested over time.

That way, assuming the market didn't go negative in any policy year (which will happen), some interest would be credited every year, unlike the example above, which only offered 2-year indexes. I think 5%-7% is a reasonable expectation for this product over time. Maybe better.

In every illustration shown in this book, we assume the index allocations were never changed to take advantage of market conditions and prospective returns.

I am very proactive every year in making index allocation change recommendations to my clients. Just as I am making changes on an ongoing basis to the portfolios I manage at Fidelity or Schwab.

The image on page 48 is taken from a recent accumulation FIA with a .95% fee (not optional) for a $306,000 lump sum purchase of non-IRA money (no RMDs). These backcasted returns are from June 26, 2004, to June 25, 2022. Why these dates? Because I ran the illustration in July and these ending July figures weren't in the software system yet.

This client was already looking at a guaranteed lifetime income FIA but wanted a 2nd one for safe growth.

NON-GUARANTEED ANNUITY CONTRACT VALUES
INDEX GROWTH PERIOD COMPARISON - MOST RECENT, HIGH, LOW

The Annual Effective Rates reflect initial allocations and application of current Index Strategy Rates to historical index returns, unless otherwise noted. The Accumulation Value reflects selected withdrawal activity.

Annual Effective Rate Most Recent: 7.96%+

Annual Effective Rate Highest: 10.26%+

Annual Effective Rate Lowest: 6.89%+

Contract Year	MOST RECENT		HIGHEST		LOWEST	
	Credited Interest Rate	Accumulation Value	Credited Interest Rate	Accumulation Value	Credited Interest Rate	Accumulation Value
At Issue		$75,000		$75,000		$75,000
1	3.28%	$77,459	3.91%	$77,931	1.65%	$76,234
2	13.56%	$87,965	25.53%	$97,827	5.09%	$80,117
3	3.63%	$91,157	3.03%	$100,790	3.50%	$82,918
4	6.00%	$96,625	10.44%	$111,312	8.50%	$89,963
5	2.62%	$99,160	2.67%	$114,285	2.35%	$92,080
6	20.86%	$119,850	16.86%	$133,553	10.91%	$102,126
7	0.06%	$119,924	0.47%	$134,182	1.96%	$104,131
8	17.10%	$140,429	17.75%	$158,006	23.46%	$128,563
9	2.56%	$144,017	2.82%	$162,455	2.55%	$131,845
10	12.05%	$161,375	22.59%	$199,159	10.74%	$146,006
	Annual Effective Rate 8 Years: 8.16%		Annual Effective Rate 8 Years: 9.76%		Annual Effective Rate 8 Years: 6.97%	
	Annual Effective Rate 10 Years: 7.96%		Annual Effective Rate 10 Years: 10.26%		Annual Effective Rate 10 Years: 6.89%	

This list of returns from that accumulation FIA uses three different indexes, each with 1, 2, and 5-year periods (diversifying in 9 ways). Other indexes are available too.

You'll notice small returns in the 1st year. That could be due to a poor market, but more likely, the cause is only 4% of the funds being invested in the one-year indexes.

Funds invested in the 2-year indexes (40%) won't get any interest credited until the end of the 2nd year. The same goes for the 5-year indexes (56%), which is why you see some very nice returns when those 5-year indexes credit interest. It was worth the wait, as you can see.

In general, the longer the index holding period, the higher the participation rate or cap is. Of course, the danger is having the market crash right before the end of the 5th year and getting no interest for that 5-year allocation.

But this particular FIA allows us to take and keep our earnings at any time during the 1-, 2-, or 5-year period and lock it in. Then on the next policy anniversary, decide how we want to reallocate those funds. That's impressive!

It's the only insurer with the ability to do that, and a reason why I like this company so much. This is a very cool feature that my clients appreciate very much. The longer the index time period, the higher the potential growth.

That illustration does not show any withdrawals, as the client won't likely need the money for over 20 years.

End of Year Credited Interest Rate[2]	End of Year Accumulation Value
0.24 %	$305,565
3.72 %	$315,767
0.38 %	$315,729
11.04 %	$349,345
20.81 %	$420,489
10.25 %	$462,065
0.32 %	$461,631
17.29 %	$539,550
0.27 %	$538,365
75.07 %	$939,915
0.09 %	$937,179
3.65 %	$967,836
0.24 %	$966,352
18.90 %	$1,145,219
35.99 %	$1,551,895
9.90 %	$1,700,049
0.13 %	$1,695,500
2.24 %	$1,726,794

So all this growth (which worked out to about 10% per year over that time) is tax deferred. There won't be any tax until the client withdraws money.

There are no annual 1099 forms going to the IRS. Who likes paying income taxes on money they aren't spending?

To be sure, I NEVER would tell one of my clients to expect 9%-10% avg. returns in ANY FIA. And when putting one of these FIAs in a written retirement income plan, I typically use a very conservative 4%-6% average return since this, like all FIAs, is a bond alternative. But you can see the potential to beat that expectation handily.

One more thing. Although the illustration returns don't show any withdrawals, the best FIAs allow you to take up to 10% of your deposit out each year from the 2nd year onward without any surrender charges or penalties. Others only allow 5%-7% annual penalty-free withdrawals.

Therefore, no matter how attractive these financial tools can be, I wouldn't invest so much in FIAs to put you in the position of needing to take more than 10% out in any year (until the end of the 5, 7, or 10-year surrender charge period). Always have a decent amount of emergency funds invested where you can access money for unexpected events. You should never pay a penalty.

Bonds Vs. BUFFER Annuities

Now let's look at the other main type of accumulation FIA, what I call BUFFER annuities. You'll see why I named them that when I describe my common-sense income/RMD withdrawal planning strategy.

This section was taken from my book, —BUFFER Annuities: No-Fee Bond-Alternatives for a Smarter Withdrawal Strategy—which is available on Amazon in paperback and KINDLE.

In the other book, there is a fuller discussion of what I call

49

BUFFER annuities and some more financial planning info that is not included in these pages. But this should suffice.

Then, I'll describe how they (or any good accumulation FIA) fit into my Required Minimum Distribution (RMD) strategy to help make the 4% rule actually work in your retirement. And maybe, just maybe, stretch that often disputed 4% rule to something closer to 5% or better so you can really enjoy your retirement.

Again, BUFFER annuities are designed for accumulation. They give you the option to pay a fee (subtracted from your account) to buy more upside when you think the markets are going to do well.

It's an option that you have at the start of every policy year. You can pay the fee on some, none, or all of the indexes you decide to allocate to.

And although you can earn stock-like average returns, I use these products as BOND ALTERNATIVES.

Dr. Wade Pfau, CFA, told Forbes magazine in 2015 that "bonds don't belong in a retirement portfolio." He still believes and teaches that to advisors across the country today. Bonds lost about 15% in 2022 as interest rates rose.

Here's the case against bonds in the traditional 60/40 portfolio. Dr. Pfau says that with the current low interest rates of virtually all bonds and the credit risks of all non-U.S. Treasuries plus interest rate risk for all bonds, bonds should play no more than a minor role in a retirement portfolio. Oh yeah, and bonds have inflation risk too. A fixed coupon rate is <u>fixed</u> and has no protection against rising prices (inflation).

The argument against bonds is still happening. Warren Buffett was none too kind to bonds either in his annual shareholder letter of February 2021, where he wrote:

"And bonds are not the place to be these days. Can you believe that the income recently available from a 10-year U.S. Treasury bond – the yield was 0.93% at yearend – had fallen 94% from the 15.8% yield available in September 1981? In certain large and important countries, such as Germany and Japan, investors earn a negative return on trillions of dollars of sovereign debt. Fixed-income investors worldwide – whether pension funds, insurance companies or retirees – face a bleak future."

That's what Warren Buffett thinks.

I mostly agree with each of them that with the recent low-interest rates of virtually all bonds and the credit risks of non-U.S. Treasuries plus interest rate risk for all bonds, bonds should play no more than a minor role in a retirement portfolio. We need to find more attractive alternatives, and our investment firm has them!

But before we get into BUFFERS, let me continue to show you more about why so many financial professionals (including yours truly) are so concerned about bonds right now.

The U.S. Aggregate Bond Index (AGG) comprises highly rated corporate bonds, government debt, and mortgage-backed debt and offered a yield of 5.4% (11/9/23). That is more than today's inflation rate of 3.2% (before taxes).

Keep in mind that bond coupon rates are fixed. If you buy $100,000 of an AAA-rated 20-year corporate bond today with a fixed coupon rate of 5%, you'll get paid $5,000 interest every year for 20 years, and then (hopefully—if you didn't buy a bond from a future Enron or similar) you'll get your $100,000 back.

What investor can live on a fixed 5% income? Inflation is not fixed—it compounds over time! Even at 2% inflation, in just 5 years, that $5,000 of fixed income would only buy $4,529 worth of "stuff" in today's dollars. And only $4,102 worth of stuff in 10 years.

Inflation is a fixed-income investor's worst enemy. That's a loser's game long-term. You can do better.

And yes, you have credit risk with most bonds too. Although defaults are historically low, not every bond will be paid back in full.

But it gets worse. Bond prices move in the opposite direction of yields. With rising rates, the Bloomberg Bond Index had lost -16.56% for the year to date (Oct. 2022).

At these historic low-interest rates, should interest rates return to more normal levels, the prices of the bonds in your portfolio will nosedive.

Let's get back to BUFFERs.

Like all FIAs, your actual returns are simply "linked" to the returns of the indexes used. The insurer uses options on 1 and 2-year indexes to get returns. There are 5 indexes, but I typically would only use 3 of them, all of them diversified into the one-year and 2-year indexes.

These three little-known products are strictly designed for tax-deferred accumulation and growth without market risk.

Your investment is backed by an A+ rated (AM BEST) insurance company. And again, your money is never invested in the markets—so your investment is never subject to market risk.

But I take that one step further and use them for my RMD and withdrawal strategies—so my clients don't end up like Jill (from a few chapters back). We want the 4% rule to actually work!

Like all accumulations FIAs, there are NO attractive guaranteed lifetime income options nor any "maybe" LTC benefits "doublers" that some other annuities may offer. Those will be discussed further in the book.

BUFFER annuities can be passive "set-it-and-forget-it" or actively managed once a year (which is what I suggest).

Why don't we begin by taking a closer look at my bond fund alternative with my client Joe?

Let's say Joe is just looking to have a slow and steady growth – without any market risk and does not want to pay any fees for more significant potential returns. That's OK, no problem

He decides to invest $100,000. Here is the range of past returns based on my suggested index allocation (for diversification) with NO FEES—zero costs.

In this allocation, I diversified with the five indexes — 50% in the one-year allocation and the rest in the 2-year indexes. That is why the biggest returns tend to be in the "even" years rather than the "odd" years.

The 2-year always has higher potential returns due to higher participation rates, BUT we have to wait 2 years to see what we earned and get the interest credited to our account.

But I like to get at least some return every year, which is why I usually put at least 25%-50% of the funds in the one-year allocation. But you can put some, all, or nothing in the one-year allocation.

Again, you get to decide precisely how you want to reallocate the funds each year. I want your account to grow safely! (I'm always happy to make recommendations).

Like previous illustrations, the left box is the ten most recent calendar years, the middle box is the best 10-year period out of the last 20 years (some 2,000 tested periods), and the box on the right is the worst 10-year period out of the last 20 years.

Again, there are no fees in the first chart below. The next 10 years will not look the same as the last 10 years. I think they won't be as good... but they could be better.

When including this CONSERVATIVE allocation inside one of my retirement income plans, I'm using very conservative average annual gains of only 4%, which is about 55% of the worst 10-year period and well below the other two boxes.

That 4% future return figure is higher than what most believe the Bond Index will provide, with less risk.

If actual returns are better than that—the RMD plan becomes better as well. Remember that since 50% of the funds are in the 2-year bucket, they never get any interest credited until the end of the 2nd year.

Now, these indexes did NOT exist 20 years ago, but backcasted using the same systematic rules-based algorithms for determining the investments within each index.

Of course, future returns are not guaranteed (other than a 0% return when markets go down) and will likely be very different than shown.

Bonds, bond mutual funds, and bond ETFs have NO guarantees at all, have more risk, and have higher expenses.

And you will notice there are pretty similar returns across the board (both good and bad) over the 10-year period in the most recent, highest, and lowest charts right below.

In Chart #1, the lowest (worst past ten years would have been 7.15% average returns, and the most recent ten years would have been 8.41%.

I would expect average annual returns of between 5.5%-7% over the next ten years.

Maybe not such exciting returns compared to stocks, are they? But they crush CD returns at any bank and will likely outperform bond funds—with less credit risk, interest rate risk, and inflation risk.

No fees and no expenses. No credit or interest rate risk either.

Let's look at the same annuity but with "some" optional fees to buy more upside and potentially better gains. Again, there are NO mandatory fees or expenses at all.

But with a 0% floor, why not take a little more risk (.5% maximum loss due to a fee) in a negative market for more upside potential?

BUFFER Chart #1

NON-GUARANTEED ANNUITY CONTRACT VALUES
INDEX GROWTH PERIOD COMPARISON - MOST RECENT, HIGH, LOW

The Annual Effective Rates reflect initial allocations and application of current Index Strategy Rates to historical index returns, unless otherwise noted. The Accumulation Value reflects selected withdrawal activity.

Annual Effective Rate Most Recent: 8.41%+

Annual Effective Rate Highest: 10.82%+

Annual Effective Rate Lowest: 7.15%+

Contract Year	MOST RECENT		HIGHEST		LOWEST	
	Credited Interest Rate	Accumulation Value	Credited Interest Rate	Accumulation Value	Credited Interest Rate	Accumulation Value
At Issue		$100,000		$100,000		$100,000
1	3.76%	$103,763	5.41%	$105,409	2.39%	$102,390
2	13.66%	$117,937	25.00%	$131,762	2.52%	$104,972
3	4.63%	$123,400	3.57%	$136,467	2.76%	$107,867
4	5.55%	$130,243	14.74%	$156,580	9.74%	$118,372
5	2.84%	$133,946	3.67%	$162,328	2.27%	$121,062
6	23.24%	$165,074	11.99%	$181,796	14.90%	$139,100
7	0.05%	$165,158	1.67%	$184,825	4.46%	$145,310
8	17.92%	$194,752	21.24%	$224,074	22.29%	$177,705
9	2.72%	$200,041	1.53%	$227,724	2.02%	$181,286
10	12.13%	$224,302	22.65%	$279,298	10.05%	$199,507
Annual Effective Rate	8.41%+		10.82%+		7.15%+	

So, Mary is OK with paying "some" fees since she pays her advisor to manage her bond money now.

In Chart #2, the returns are based on my suggested index allocation (diversification). Half of the indexes have NO FEES, and the other half (optional fee) cost 1% annually, for an overall net fee cost of 0.5%.

The optional fees allow for higher potential returns (better participation rates/caps/spreads) – while your worst return is 0% in any year—except for any optional fee charged for purchasing more upside potential (buying more options).

Again, I split 50/50 between the one and 2-year allocations. Recall there are higher potential returns in the 2-year allocation, which is why you will notice the bigger returns in the "even" years, as the 2-year allocations only get the interest credited at the end of the 2nd year.

Earnings would be smoother but likely lower if 100% of the funds were in the 1-yr buckets.

Again, there is no interest credited to any allocation in the 2-year indexes until the end of the 2nd year. But I like to get at least some return every year, so I usually put at least 25%-50% of the principal in the one-year allocation.

You get to decide however you want to allocate the funds every single year.

Again, the left box is the most recent 10 calendar years, the middlebox is the best 10-year period out of the last 20 years (some 2,000 tested periods), and the right box is the worst 10-year period out of the previous 20 years.

The returns shown below are NET of the 0.5% annual fees (optional) returns the investor gets to keep. The next ten years will not look the same as the last ten years. I think they won't be as good... but they could be better.

In Chart #2, the lowest (worst past ten years) would have been 8.16% average returns, and the most recent calendar ten years would have been 9.64%.

Since I don't think the next ten years will be as good as the last ten, I would expect average annual NET returns of between 6.5%-8% over the next ten years, even after the 0.5% optional annual fee (only 50% of the acct. at 1% fee).

Again, in a retirement income plan, I would conservatively use a 5% average annual return with this design. I'm pretty sure we'll do better than that, though.

Keep in mind that since 50% of the funds are in the 2-year bucket, they never get any interest credited until the end of the 2nd year. And again, no sequence of return risk at all.

These past returns are a lot more exciting when compared to bond funds. In fact, even the worst 10-year period above (right column) beat the total returns of the S&P 500 index from 2000-2011, which were under 3% annualized. And the index had four big negative years to deal with too.

BUFFER Chart #2

NON-GUARANTEED ANNUITY CONTRACT VALUES
INDEX GROWTH PERIOD COMPARISON - MOST RECENT, HIGH, LOW

The Annual Effective Rates reflect initial allocations and application of current Index Strategy Rates to historical index returns, unless otherwise noted. The Accumulation Value reflects strategy fees and selected withdrawal activity.

Contract Year	MOST RECENT		HIGHEST		LOWEST	
	Credited Interest Rate*	Accumulation Value	Credited Interest Rate*	Accumulation Value	Credited Interest Rate*	Accumulation Value
At Issue		$100,000		$100,000		$100,000
1	4.82%	$104,568	6.91%	$106,662	2.39%	$102,141
2	15.63%	$120,130	31.09%	$139,033	4.37%	$105,843
3	5.47%	$126,395	4.30%	$144,877	3.00%	$108,796
4	6.87%	$134,146	17.07%	$168,221	11.37%	$120,301
5	3.41%	$138,388	4.36%	$175,139	4.40%	$125,292
6	28.17%	$176,325	15.84%	$201,432	16.75%	$146,329
7	0.02%	$175,909	1.99%	$204,963	3.96%	$150,556
8	22.58%	$214,239	24.45%	$253,312	27.51%	$190,816
9	4.65%	$223,667	3.06%	$260,446	2.52%	$195,150
10	13.03%	$250,985	28.90%	$333,456	13.30%	$219,592
Annual Effective Rate	10.13%+		13.31%+		8.68%+	
Net Annual Effective Rate	9.64%^		12.80%^		8.18%^	

And finally, Michael has NO issue with paying fees (to buy more options) for the potential for much greater returns or waiting 2 years to get interest credited to his account. Since his downside is protected (0% floor), he's willing to pay the fee on all indexes to get the enhanced potential.

Here are the returns based on my suggested index allocation (diversification), with ALL the indexes having (optional) fees costing 1% annually.

To be frank, most of my clients will and have liked this option the best so far. They tell me, "If a 1% fee is my worst downside when the markets tank, why not reach for the moon and get the highest returns I can over time?" In this case, his worst year is a -1% due to the fee.

The 3rd chart has all the funds invested in the 2-year allocations, so no interest is credited to the policy until the end of every 2nd year (see 0% on the odd years).

You always get to decide however you want to allocate your funds each year. I'm always happy and dedicated to helping with recommendations. Again, I am going to make the assumption that the next ten years will not look the same as the last ten years. I don't think they will be as good... but they could be even better.

Like before, the left box is the most recent ten calendar years, the middle is the best 10-year period out of the last 20 years (some 2,000 tested daily periods), and the box on the right is the worst 10-year period out of the 20 years.

BUFFER Chart #3

NON-GUARANTEED ANNUITY CONTRACT VALUES
INDEX GROWTH PERIOD COMPARISON - MOST RECENT, HIGH, LOW

The Annual Effective Rates reflect initial allocations and application of current Index Strategy Rates to historical index returns, unless otherwise noted. The Accumulation Value reflects strategy fees and selected withdrawal activity.

Contract Year	MOST RECENT		HIGHEST		LOWEST	
	Credited Interest Rate*	Accumulation Value	Credited Interest Rate*	Accumulation Value	Credited Interest Rate*	Accumulation Value
At Issue		$100,000		$100,000		$100,000
1	0.00%	$100,000	0.00%	$100,000	0.00%	$100,000
2	20.19%	$118,185	58.16%	$156,160	11.13%	$109,130
3	0.00%	$118,185	0.00%	$156,160	0.00%	$109,130
4	16.58%	$135,414	26.96%	$195,144	15.15%	$123,476
5	0.00%	$135,414	0.00%	$195,144	0.00%	$123,476
6	40.41%	$187,424	28.10%	$246,072	24.06%	$150,714
7	0.00%	$187,424	0.00%	$246,072	0.00%	$150,714
8	28.89%	$237,815	31.34%	$318,276	44.79%	$215,203
9	0.00%	$237,815	0.00%	$318,276	0.00%	$215,203
10	22.21%	$285,669	46.31%	$459,312	28.39%	$271,993
Annual Effective Rate	11.97%+		17.33%+		11.43%+	
Net Annual Effective Rate	11.08%^		16.47%^		10.52%^	

The returns shown above are NET of the 1% annual fees (optional)—returns the investor gets to keep. This time, there is 100% in the 2-year allocation, which is why the only returns are in the "even" years.

This is a more AGGRESSIVE allocation. Those are much higher returns than what most believe the Bond Index or most bond funds will provide and are closer to equity-type returns with much less risk.

Using all fees, I'd project something like an 8%-9% avg. annual return over 10 years. That's 3 times the total return of the S&P 500 from 2000-2011 (including dividends). However, even a 5% average return will likely crush bonds.

Do you see the 44% gain in the LOWEST column (right) in year 4? And then the other 2-year gains of 24% and 28% in years 6 and 10?

In real life, for more "aggressive" investors, I'd probably design this to have 50% in the one-year bucket the first year only and then switch to 100% in the 2-year buckets. So, I'd have a 2-year bucket (50%) coming due with interest earned every single year. You'd still get higher total participation rates but should earn interest almost every year, which would be helpful when taking RMDs or distributions.

Again, these returns assume we never make educated changes in the indexes based on the economy and markets. With some changes made over time, I'd suspect the returns could be even greater.

Remember to think of this as a "Principal Protected" account – where your worst return is 0%! You can never experience a loss induced by the market. Yet you have plenty of upside. Just look at the growth in all scenarios.

The only "loss" you can ever have is up to a 1% reduction in account value if you decide to put 100% of the funds in the index managed by Fidelity (1 or 2 years) and the index's return was less than 0%.

I forgot to mention one HUGE fact regarding the optional fee of 1% should you ever decide to take advantage of gaining more upside. Oh, this is cool.

If you use it and at the end of your 10 years you paid more in fees than you got in gains, they would bring you back to even (as if you never paid the fees at all).

Let me explain it this way. Say you invest $100,000. If you paid 1% in fees for 100% of your index allocation every year (AGGRESSIVE allocation), and each and every one of the indexes went down every single year at the end of the ten years, you could actually walk away with your entire $100,000 back.

In other words, they would refund all fees paid to get you back to where you started. It is not likely to ever be needed or used, but it is guaranteed. I think that is very fair, don't you?

One client told me that's like gambling with no risk of loss. Try to get that guarantee in Las Vegas!

Of course, this is not for everyone or every situation for sure. No financial strategy or product is or ever will be.

But I believe that it is certainly worth exploring for at least a portion of your bond portfolio, given the current state of interest rates and their foreseeable future. Of course, it is an attractive CD alternative too.

The main point of this chapter and charts was to show how your principal is protected and that you have the advantage of the reset mechanism to help you when the markets crash (in that your indexes don't have to get back to the pre-crash levels to start making returns again).

Unlike the stock market, market volatility is truly your friend with BUFFER annuities (and ALL FIAs).

Why is that?

Again, because of the lock-in and reset. When the markets crash, your FIA is protected by the 0% floor. Not only that, but the indexes also reset on your policy anniversary, and your future gains are determined by the lower levels of the indexes due to the lock-in and reset.

As I wrote earlier, financial products are like golf clubs. They simply help you get around the golf course with as good a score as you are capable of. They are a means to an end. A tool to help you achieve your financial goals.

You don't want only to have a putter or a driver and use that ONE club for every shot you make over the 18 holes.

That's why you carry a full bag of clubs. Financial products are no different.

All annuities, mutual funds, ETFs, stocks, bonds, and insurance should be more than just products. They should be SOLUTIONS to financial problems or worries. If they don't solve a problem, then you don't need them. Period.

If you are not a golfer, think about household tools. Again, if you need to make a hole in the wall, you use a drill, not a hammer. If you need to cut a piece of wood in half, a hammer won't do a good job, but a saw will!

As a financial advisor for the past 25+ years, I've been using the "right" golf club or financial tool to solve client problems and fears or to take advantage of opportunities. So I use hammers when that tool solves a particular problem and a saw for another financial problem.

Clients want personalized solutions, not products.
Part of my job is uncovering clients' fears, doubts, and uncertainties. The things that keep them up at night.

Accumulation annuities can solve the problem inherent in bonds. Rising interest rates can cause the value of bonds to fall. Bonds also have credit risk and definite maturities, which produces reinvestment-rate risk. Bonds also have fixed coupon rates. FIAs don't have those issues. But no financial product is perfect. Nothing ever is. And even if someone were not too worried about the bonds in their portfolio, I'd venture to guess that the returns (without bond risks) will be higher in them over time versus bonds.

As we'll see in a moment, BUFFER annuities can solve problems with Required Minimum Distributions (RMDs) when stock portfolios are falling and hold their value when interest rates rise and as bonds lose value.

January 20, 2021. Here's Morningstar's take on the likely future of bonds going forward: "Bond-market bulls are few and far between, too. While a 60/40 portfolio composed of U.S. large caps and investment-grade bonds has been tough to beat over the past decade, most of the firms in our survey are forecasting constrained returns for those asset classes going forward."

It's worth noting that in playing hockey, you want to skate to where the puck is going—not where it's been. That's what the pro players do.

It's the same with investing. The 30-year bull market in bonds (rising bond values, with interest rates declining over that time) is probably over. Let's look forward and skate to where interest rates and bond prices are likely going to be down the road.

Comments like the above and similar ones from JPMorgan and Bank of America (essentially saying that the "60/40 portfolio is dead") can be a problem for folks in or near retirement. So, we need to find appropriate solutions to make their retirement income both larger and safer.

But as I wrote earlier, it's not just the bond component of the 60/40 portfolio that is becoming worrisome. So are equities.

I might add at this point that Index Universal Life (IUL) insurance policies (or even whole life insurance) could also be great alternatives to bonds. IULs work in the same manner that FIAs do with a 0% floor but have higher caps and participation rates, and, of course, a valuable tax-free death benefit.

I call IULs my TRIPLE ZERO™ plans as they are ROTH alternatives – 1) ZERO income/contribution limits 2) ZERO market risk and 3) ZERO income taxes when you play by the IRS rules. They can be 100% TAX-FREE!

You can buy my book —_TAX-FREE Millionaire_— on KINDLE or paperback at Amazon, which only explains TRIPLE ZERO™ plans or the expanded version —_Get Me to ZERO_— which describes <u>seven</u> strategies for a tax-free retirement (including the full description of TRIPLE ZERO™ plans).

Life insurance cannot be held inside an IRA, so we have to use non-IRA money to fund one. And to be fully tax-free, we must follow the IRS rules about funding the policy over a minimum of 4-5 years (rather than a lump sum premium made into a BUFFER annuity).

Like BUFFER annuities, only a few IUL policies allow you to pay a fee to buy more options and get more upside, but they are available.

But life insurance does not have RMDs, so although you can take tax-free distributions from your specially designed IUL policy to help fund your retirement lifestyle, but it doesn't solve the RMD rule issues.

Our firm has other non-insurance-based bond-alternative and stock strategies, too, which are beyond the scope of this book. In my portfolios, I take as much risk off the table as possible with many overlooked investment strategies.

Before we switch gears and discuss FIAs that offer attractive guaranteed lifetime income to add another risk-free and guaranteed income stream to your retirement years, let's explore my powerful withdrawal strategy.

My BUFFER/Accumulation FIA Withdrawal Strategy

So far, we've seen the past returns of the bond-alternative accumulation and BUFFER FIAs and learned how they work.

You've seen why many financial professionals think that the traditional 60/40 portfolios are "dead." Most of the concern has been on the bond side of the portfolio. Further along in the book, you'll see Vanguard's stock and bond predictions for the coming decade, which make both sides of your portfolio look suspect.

You've learned about (or have been reminded about) the "4% rule," as a rule of thumb of how much you can take out of your savings each year, adjusted for inflation.

However, no matter what returns you AVERAGE over your retirement, it's the <u>sequence</u> of those returns that will largely determine the success or failure of the 4% rule or whatever withdrawal rate you deem appropriate.

And I haven't even written about tax-smart portfolio strategies in this book! Most folks spend too much time worrying about their returns and not enough on being tax-savvy. We all need to pay our fair share, but why pay more to the IRS than you need to?

Now it's time to see how I use BUFFER annuities in client portfolios regarding smart Required Minimum Distribution (RMD) and withdrawal strategies.

It's time to learn how to replace a good portion of your bonds with these BUFFERs to increase your overall returns while decreasing interest rates and credit risks.

Let's begin with a quick analogy. You are on the top floor of a 55-story building, and you want to get down to the lobby safely. You have two choices to get there. Yes, there is a 3rd choice (the stairwell), but most of us wouldn't even consider this option unless there's a fire.

The elevator on the right has three cables securing it. The elevator on the left has only one cable. Which elevator are you going to get on? Would you take the first elevator whose doors opened, or would you wait for the elevator on the right with the three cables to take you down?

Most of us (except those thrill-seekers), would wait for the more secure elevator. I certainly would.

Well, think of the three cables as a thoughtfully crafted (skating to where the puck is going to be) portfolio of equities, a diverse fixed-income strategy (more than just bonds), and BUFFER annuities that can take advantage of stock market volatility with the protection of a 0% floor.

Maybe 2 strategies for each cable for more diversification. In our investment advisory firm, we like to use a number of alternative bond strategies that I would call "fixed-income" rather than simply a bond index(s).

We do that to minimize interest rate risk, duration risk, and even credit risk that is inherent in bonds. In fact, we can use several different equity strategies as well to reduce market risk. They have a great track record.

Our firm manages some $8.5 BILLION in over 50,000 client accounts in all 50 states. Unlike most firms that focus on the portfolio's stock side, we believe that the fixed-income side needs just as much attention. Maybe more today.

But as mentioned earlier, our stock/fixed income portfolio design and investment management are beyond the scope of this book.

Think of the elevator with just one cable as the typical 60/40 portfolio at Vanguard or anywhere else. Make sure to take a look at their projections in a later chapter.

Now, neither Vanguard nor any other investment firm can truly tell the future, but they certainly have the weight and experience of hundreds of professional market analysts and academic researchers behind them.

Anyway, let's review Required Minimum Distributions (RMDs) for traditional IRAs, 401(k)s, 403(b)s, 457s, SEPs, SIMPLEs, and other deductible retirement plans.

The IRS allowed you to deduct your retirement contributions (within limits) while you were working.

Now at age 73 (new law starting in 2023—it used to be age 70.5 and then 72), they want to start collecting the taxes on both your contributions and the investment earnings your accounts have earned tax deferred for decades.

They make you take out some money every year from age 73 (whether you need the funds or not) - so they can finally TAX you on it.

The first-year RMD is about 3.77%. If you have $100,000 total in your IRAs on December 31st, then you'd have to withdraw $3,774 the following year. The next year, the percentage of withdrawal goes up and does so every year going forward.

Let me repeat that. Each year, as you get older, the RMD percentage you must take out of your IRA grows a bit. For example, when you're 85, you must take out about 6.25%. At age 92, it's about 9.3% of your IRA balance(s).

The good thing about RMDs and IRAs is that the IRS doesn't care which IRA you take the RMD from (if you have more than one). You can take 100% of your total RMD from one IRA and not touch the others or take it out pro-rata from all of them or anything in between.

Keep in mind that RMDs are calculated separately if you are married. So, you'll have your own RMD and your spouse will have their own RMD.

Of course, there are no RMDs if you own any ROTHs.

Please note that the IRS looks at 401(k)s, 403(b)s, and 457 plans differently for some reason. You must take the RMD from that account only. You cannot take a 401(k) based RMD from an IRA account. Crazy.

Well, that is the government for you! So, simply roll your 401(k) into an IRA! Anyway, that's just another reason why I generally recommend rolling over your savings from a 401(k), 403(b), etc., to an IRA.

So, knowing that you have complete flexibility in where you take your IRA RMDs from; this is how we use BUFFER annuities as part of an intelligent withdrawal strategy.

By the way, the withdrawal strategy works even if you are not age 73 yet and are just withdrawing funds from your savings (IRAs or brokerage accounts) to fund your retirement lifestyle. The principle and results work exactly the same.

The strategy revolves around "buy low" and "sell high." Or at least don't sell (and withdraw) your RMD or lifestyle money after the market has crashed. Why?

Because once you've withdrawn (sold your stocks) to take your RMD or make a withdrawal for any reason, those shares of stocks can never recover along with the market—since they are no longer in the account (you spent them).

You'll recall that any accumulation and/or BUFFER annuities can never go down because of the markets. ZERO is your hero in a market crash.

So, here is my nearly foolproof yet straightforward strategy to make sure you never have to sell stocks, mutual funds, and ETFs in a down market to fund your RMD or lifestyle withdrawal. It just takes a little discipline to make the strategy work.

When the previous year's stock market ends higher, you take your **total** RMD (including any RMD necessary from your BUFFER/accumulations annuity) from the stock market account. You leave the FIA alone that year.

Again, we want to sell stocks, funds, etc., when they are higher, not when they lost money (i.e., more than 5%). Take the profits when the market gives them to you. Don't watch them evaporate in the next market crash.

The market goes up 3 out of every 4 years on average, so

you'll be taking total RMDs from this account most years.

On that one out of every 4 years, on average, when the market drops (ends lower), we take the **total** RMD from the BUFFER annuity (since it doesn't get any of the market losses) and let our stock accounts recover. We don't sell when the stocks are low. We let them rise in value again.

If the market stays down for a second year, you take the total RMD out of the BUFFER annuity again. And let your stocks recover.

It hardly ever happens that the market is down three years in a row (2000, 2001, and 2002), but if it's necessary, then take the 3rd **total** RMD from the BUFFER annuity too.

If you have a number of good years in the market, keep taking your withdrawals from the stock accounts and let the BUFFER annuity grow until the next time you tap it for income or RMDs.

This is what Norma (my beautiful bride) and I have done. We took 40% of her IRA money (from her 401(k) rollover) out of our firm's managed account at Schwab and then put it into the 2 BUFFER annuities that I described earlier in the book.

We used 2 BUFFER annuities for index diversification, and it made sense with the amount of dollars she invested.

With the money remaining at Schwab, we are 80% in

equity ETFs and some mutual funds and the other 20% in our firm's alternative fixed-income strategies – for better returns than bond index funds (with less risk).

So essentially, we now have 48% in stocks – ETFs and mutual funds - (with some hedging for protection), 40% in BUFFER annuities, and 12% in our firm's fixed-income alternatives. And we sleep very well at night.

I expect the returns in the BUFFER annuities will do almost as well as the stock market over the next decade since they have the 0% floor protection when the market goes down and the very valuable "lock-in and reset" features.

I'm projecting 6%-7% average NET returns in our BUFFER annuities (using my preferred index allocations), which are higher than Vanguard's stock projections for the U.S. markets (let alone their forecast for the bond markets).

I believe they will undoubtedly beat the projected returns of the bond indexes that Vanguard made. For that matter, so will our firm's alternate fixed-income strategies. That's not to say that what we are doing for ourselves would be the right thing for you or anyone else. For example, you might want to take more or less risk.

It's seldom that I recommend something to a client that we don't own ourselves. Of course, there are some ideas or strategies that are not in line with our own goals and circumstances. So, I don't implement those in our own plan since they don't fit the bill for our financial planning.

And you know what else we did? We took the sequence of returns risk off the table—no "Jill" scenarios. That about wraps it up for BUFFER annuities.

As you have seen, BUFFER and accumulation annuities can have excellent returns (especially if you opt to pay the small fee to buy more upside)—without taking any market risk.

Although they are not hedge funds, they are certainly an appropriate alternative investment instead of bonds, bond mutual funds, and bond ETFs, which all carry interest rate risk and credit risk—while currently suffering from meager returns along the way.

Investors and retirees will have a hard time getting by on 3%-5% fixed interest rates. Even if rates go up (as they should), then the value of the bonds will fall. Just like a seesaw, when one goes up, the other goes down. And when one side goes down, the other goes up.

Getting average annual returns of 5%, 6%, or higher over time versus bonds (especially if fixed income is 40%-60% of one's portfolio) can literally rescue a retiree's future.

Those returns might even beat a conservative investor's stock portfolio's returns and do so without the sequence of returns risk. Of course, that potential outperformance would come from BUFFER annuities having the 0% floor to protect from market crashes and recessions and the unique lock-in and index reset features.

You will see Vanguard's market predictions for the coming decade of equity returns in the 3%-5%. Maybe it's time to consider taking some of your profits in the stock market off the table, too.

BUFFER annuities have no embedded fees or expenses. They are less expensive than the cheapest mutual funds or ETFs while offering more diversification than single stocks. Who doesn't like 0% expenses?

You only pay an optional fee if you want higher potential returns, and you get to make that decision every policy anniversary. You've seen the advantages and results of paying these optional fees in BUFFER Charts #2 and #3.

And you learned about the 4% rule (if you hadn't known about it already) and why so many market professionals think that it won't work in the future for 60/40 portfolios.

Of course, you'll have to come to your own conclusions about those projections based on your thinking.

And then, there is the tax deferral inherent in every type of annuity. I've hardly mentioned tax deferral because about 75% of my clients put IRA-type money into their BUFFER annuities.

But using non-qualified (the IRS term for non-IRA-type money) makes sense as well. You can then control the timing of your taxation. Tax deferral is a very good thing, as you can see from my chart on page 80.

The chart shows the power of putting off paying taxes. Although money does not double every year (at least not for 20 years in a row), the chart below illustrates my point nicely. The tax-deferred account is on the left, while the taxed annually (at only a 15% tax rate) is on the right.

Of course, taxes will eventually be due when the funds are withdrawn from the account. But wouldn't you rather pay 15% taxes on $1,048,576 and net **$891,290 after tax**?

Even at a 50% tax rate on the $1,000,000, you'd still net over $500,000 after tax. That's over $280,000 more!

That's more than **$220,514**. I'd opt to pay taxes on 4 times as many gains every day of the week. Wouldn't you? Even if taxes go to 75%, tax deferral still makes sense!

And most importantly, I hope you have seen that using BUFFER annuities as part of your withdrawal or RMD strategy will make your money last longer (or leave a more significant legacy to family or the charities you care about)—while taking market-induced stress away.

You'll sell and withdraw your stocks when they ended the previous year higher and not touch them (withdrawing funds from your BUFFER instead) when the markets closed the last year lower—selling high, not selling low.

This way, you let your stocks recover along with the market. It's not actually a loss until you take it (sell). That is why accountants call it "unrealized losses."

Year	Uninterrupted	Taxed Annually
1	$2.00	$1.85
2	$4.00	$3.42
3	$8.00	$6.33
4	$16.00	$11.71
5	$32.00	$21.67
6	$64.00	$40.09
7	$128.00	$74.17
8	$256.00	$137.21
9	$512.00	$253.83
10	$1,024.00	$469.59
11	$2,048.00	$868.74
12	$4,096.00	$1,607.17
13	$8,192.00	$2,973.26
14	$16,384.00	$5,500.53
15	$32,768.00	$10,175.97
16	$65,536.00	$18,825.55
17	$131,072.00	$34,827.27
18	$262,144.00	$64,430.44
19	$524,288.00	$119,196.32
20	$1,048,576.00	$220,513.19

This strategy is the way to take much of the sequence of returns risk off the table during your retirement. And as you'll recall, it is not the "average" return that you achieve in retirement; it is the <u>sequence</u> of those returns.

When your returns are excellent when you begin to take withdrawals from your account, the sequence of returns is your friend. However, the opposite is also true, and a "bad sequence" can ruin a retirement forever. There's no going back. This strategy significantly reduces that risk.

FIAs That Offer Guaranteed Lifetime Income

I believe this type of FIA has larger annual sales than the accumulation-type FIAs. So that I don't repeat "guaranteed income annuity" over and over in this section, I'll refer to these types of FIAs as "GIs."

Unlike accumulation FIAs, GIs focus more on generating the highest possible lifetime income than making the account larger. It's really an income play.

Yes, the account will grow until the guaranteed income stream is turned on at some point (either right away or at some point in the future). That was the reason the client bought the product—to have another stream of income that would last throughout their lifetime.

Unlike a Single Premium Immediate Annuity (SPIA), you do not immediately give up complete control of and access to your cash with a GI.

With GIs, there are really two account values. One is the cash surrender value, which grows as the indexes earn returns (and you have some access to). The account value (no surrender charges after the surrender period or upon death) is also the lump sum death benefit. This account value will slowly reduce over time as the lifetime income is withdrawn every month or year. I'll show this happening in the image on page 84.

The more important value in GIs is the income base (the

insurers have different names for it), which is the value that determines either the initial (rising over time to help against inflation) or the guaranteed level of income once the policy owner decides to turn on the lifetime income.

Essentially, there are two types of GIs. One type is performance-based, which gives you the highest potential income (not guaranteed) based on the performance of the indexes chosen. These will be discussed next.

The other type of GI is designed to offer the highest guaranteed lifetime income (joint or single), even if the indexes earn 0% every single year. Because of the higher guaranteed income, performance-based GIs will always show a higher income stream, with the additional benefit of a growing income. I'll give an example of a great high-level guaranteed income at the end of this chapter.

The income base, or whatever the insurer calls it, is a "phantom" value. You can't take the value out of the contract except as lifetime income. Some policies also use the income base as a 2nd death benefit option, if that value is taken out over five years or longer. For many survivors (usually children), which could be enticing.

The other part of the guaranteed income calculation is the payout factor. Payout factors are guaranteed (part of the contract) and are based on the age of the younger (in a joint lifetime income policy). The older the age(s) when you decide to turn on the income stream, the higher the payout factor will be.

A typical factor for a single 65-year-old would be 5% of the income base amount or so. A 65-year-old couple's joint income factor would be lower (say 4.5%), as two people are expected to live longer than one.

Besides the underlying indexes used in the product, the biggest difference between the various GIs is how the benefit base is calculated. There is a multitude of ways that insurers can use to increase the income base.

Years ago, the main way income bases were calculated was a "roll-up." While the account value was growing by whatever the various indexes earned, the income base would grow by a guaranteed percentage. With a 6% roll-up, the income base would double in 12 years, and the income stream would be based on that number.

So if the deposit to the GI was $100,000 a dozen years ago, no matter what the indexes earned along the way, that 52-year-old couple opting for a joint lifetime income in year 13 would have known back then that their joint lifetime income would be based on the factor of 4.5% and the income base guaranteed to grow to $200,000 at that time. So, their income would start off at $9,000 per year.

Perhaps the indexes earned $45,000 over that time (remember this is a bond alternative, not a stock fund), but that doesn't always figure into the income base.

Maybe that $9,000 figure is not very exciting, but if the 4% rule was applied to an account value of $145,000, then that would imply a beginning income of only $5,800 per year. Much less exciting, isn't it?

Using the 4% rule of growing the income by the amount of inflation each year, if we use an average of 3% annual inflation, it will take 14 years to catch up to the $9,000.

And what if that $9,000 initial income could grow every year based on what the indexes earned (which are the GIs that I typically recommend)? The 4% rule would never catch up to the GI income—and never, ever run out.

This image describes perfectly how most GIs work. A client invests $200,000 and lets the account grow "X" years, then begins taking growing income (shaded columns).

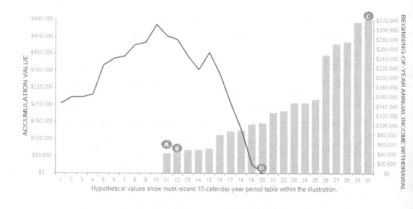

Hypothetical values show most recent 10-calendar-year period table within the illustration.

This GI illustration shows $200,000 going in as a lump sum, growing to almost $450,000 over 11 years, and having an initial joint lifetime income of about $50,000 based on the assumed growth of the indexes used via backcasting. That growth came from a mixture of 1, 2, and 5-year indexes as described earlier with its sister accumulation FIA. The longer the term, the bigger the upside potential.

In this case, the guaranteed joint lifetime income would only be $14,000/year. That assumes they got a 0% return every year for 30+ years, which is the worst-case scenario in every FIA. Thirty years of ZEROs? That is not possible.

If you believe the market is going to go down for 30 years then you should not buy an FIA. But if that's the case, you should consider getting out of the stock market entirely because at least FIAs have the protection of a 0% floor.

I would not use that $50,000 income number in any written income plan that I would do for a client. I usually split the difference between the guaranteed $14,000 and the illustrated $50,000, which in this case would be $32,000. I think it would actually be higher than that, but my clients (and I) like conservative projections.

You can see the columns quadrupling over time, indicating incredible growing income that will last as long as either one of them is alive. That's great. In my projections, I never use income growth like that, either. I typically use a 3%-4% average annual income growth from this GI.

How does the income grow? Well, in this particular GI, it grows by 150% of whatever the indexes earned the year before. So, if the indexes earn 4%, then the income amount rises by 1.5 times that account growth (6%). When you see the columns get much taller in one year, it is because the 5-year indexes are getting their interest credited. A 5-year index earning even 20% over that time will increase the portion of the PIV by 30%, thereby increasing the annual future income proportionately. This is a performance-based GI.

But for some folks, the disturbing part of the above image is the solid line that rises and then falls to zero in year 20, meaning there is no money left in the account. I get that.

Example. Hypothetical Values Over the Last 19 Years for a contract issued on 9/12/2004

Contract Year	Age	Premium	End of Year Credited Interest Rate	End of Year Accumulation Value	End of Year Pre-MVA Cash Surrender Value	End of Year Guaranteed Minimum Value	*End of Year PIV Credit	End of Year Protected Income Value	Lifetime Income Withdrawal
9/12/2004	61	$200,000							
9/11/2005	61 - 62	$0	1.79 %	$203,584	$183,226	$178,938	2.69 %	$287,527	$0
9/11/2006	62 - 63	$0	3.05 %	$209,785	$188,807	$182,964	4.58 %	$300,690	$0
9/11/2007	63 - 64	$0	1.98 %	$213,942	$195,222	$187,080	3.06 %	$309,877	$0
9/11/2008	64 - 65	$0	5.03 %	$224,710	$207,857	$191,290	7.53 %	$333,222	$0
9/11/2009	65 - 66	$0	18.71 %	$266,764	$250,091	$195,594	26.50 %	$421,533	$0
9/11/2010	66 - 67	$0	7.33 %	$286,314	$271,998	$199,994	10.73 %	$466,760	$0
9/11/2011	67 - 68	$0	0.53 %	$287,840	$277,046	$204,494	0.77 %	$470,345	$0
9/11/2012	68 - 69	$0	11.91 %	$322,132	$314,079	$209,095	18.28 %	$556,331	$0
9/11/2013	69 - 70	$0	1.99 %	$328,536	$324,430	$213,800	2.82 %	$572,002	$0
9/11/2014	70 - 71	$0	52.16 %	$499,888	$499,888	$218,611	74.99 %	$1,000,921	$0
9/11/2015	71 - 72	$0	0.00 %	$449,842	$449,842	$172,357	0.00 %	$900,714	$50,046
9/11/2016	72 - 73	$0	2.28 %	$408,908	$408,908	$125,063	3.41 %	$827,793	$50,046
9/11/2017	73 - 74	$0	1.58 %	$362,796	$362,796	$74,956	2.11 %	$738,288	$51,757
9/11/2018	74 - 75	$0	13.17 %	$350,615	$350,615	$22,464	20.34 %	$758,696	$52,986
9/11/2019	75 - 76	$0	33.26 %	$382,541	$382,541	$0	46.98 %	$912,972	$63,555
9/11/2020	76 - 77	$0	5.35 %	$305,087	$305,087	$0	8.02 %	$746,576	$92,945
9/11/2021	77 - 78	$0	1.67 %	$208,208	$208,208	$0	2.05 %	$511,405	$100,294
9/11/2022	78 - 79	$0	1.40 %	$107,072	$107,072	$0	2.09 %	$264,791	$102,610
9/11/2023	79 - 80	$0	0.52 %	$2,346	$2,346	$0	0.65 %	$5,810	$104,737
		$200,000							$668,977

But keep in mind that this GI was <u>bought</u> for a guaranteed joint lifetime income, not for a potential legacy. This goes back to my analogy of using the right household tool.

The image directly preceding this paragraph shows a hypothetical last 19 years on that policy issued on Sept. 12, 2004. I selected 3 indexes—each covering 1-, 2-, and 5-year index crediting periods with a deposit of $200,000. The interest credited at the end of each year is in the 4th column. Again, only interest in the one-year bucket gets credited in the first year. In year 2, you get more one-year interest, and the 2-year interest is credited. A good chunk of the funds is allocated to the 5-year indexes, so they don't get any interest credited until the end of each 5-year period. That's why every 5th year looks so good.

The 5th column shows how the accumulation value grows, while the next column shows the surrender value (after the penalty) should one decide to withdraw all the funds at once.

Recall there is usually a percentage that you can withdraw every year without any penalty. In this GI, that percentage is 10% from the 2nd year through the 10th year. After that, there are no surrender charges.

The next column shows the absolute worst-case scenario possible with getting 0% returns every single year, the highest fees allowed by the contract on top of the early withdrawal surrender penalty, as well as taking the full income shown in the far right column.

The next column shows the income base interest credit that this insurer calls the Protected Income Value (PIV).

As written before, the PIV interest rate credit is 150% of whatever the actual index earns and was credited to your accumulation value. So, this interest credited to your PIV value is 1.5 times what is credited to your account value. Again, the PIV value is a phantom value. Its main purpose is to determine what the lifetime income would be, multiplied by a payout factor when this couple decides to turn on the lifetime income. The PIV value also determines the death benefit should the children decide to take the much larger figure (than the remaining account value) over a 5-year period, as opposed to a lump sum.

The joint lifetime income, in this case, is 5% of the PIV value the year prior to turning on the income. The $50,000 shown (not guaranteed) is 5% of the $1,000,000 PIV. If the GI never had a positive return thereafter (all zeros year 12 and beyond), that would be the minimum lifetime income. In an income plan, I would conservatively project $32,000 as the first-year income rather than the $50,000 shown.

However, you'll notice how the initial income grows by 1.5 times whatever the indexes earn. Think of it as an inflation fighter. The initial income could easily double every 12-15 years (although in my written income plans I only use a very conservative growth of 3%-4%).

Not shown in that chart is the accumulation value going to zero about year 20 or so. Why? Well, look at the accumulation value of about $2,000 in the 19th year and compare it to the $104,000 income being taken out. At $104,000 withdrawals, the account will go to zero the following year. But the income will never stop. It's for life.

Since this is a joint guaranteed lifetime income, as long as either spouse is alive, the income will continue to flow and even increase by 1.5 times whatever interest is credited to the indexes each year.

But once there is no accumulation value left, besides the surviving spouse continuing to enjoy that income for as long as they live, there is no death benefit for heirs.

If it's a guaranteed lifetime income that is desired and not a long-term legacy, then the account value falls to zero over a 20-year period (as opposed to losing control immediately with a SPIA) is not much of a concern. We needed to cut a piece of wood, so we used a saw. Does this make sense to you? Rising income that would last over both lives was the goal here.

For years, that was the best-selling GI on the market, and many of my clients opted for it. Now that insurance company has come out with a sister product that in many ways work similarly but appeal to those who are focused on generating the highest potential income.

Some GIs have no fees, and some have required fees (usually to increase the payout factor or to buy more upside to increase the caps or participation rates). The product just described has no fees at all by contract.

Like the GI just described, it has the same indexes and crediting periods. Like that GI, you have the option for whatever the index(es) earns in any year your account gets credited with 150% of that interest. If your indexes earn 5% in one year, your account value goes up by 7.5%.

However, this sister product does have a "potential" fee, which has never been charged so far. However, this product also gives you the option to increase your PIV and lifetime income even more. How?

This GI allows you to choose each year if you'd like your income base to increase by 250% rather than 150%. What do you give up for that huge PIV income improvement?

Example: Hypothetical Values Over the Last 19 Years for a contract issued on 9/12/2004

Contract Year	Age	Premium	End of Year Indexed Interest Rate	End of Year Credited Interest Rate	End of Year Accumulation Value	End of Year Pre-MVA Cash Value	End of Year Guaranteed Minimum Value	End of Year Protected Income Value Interest Credit	Protected Income Value	Lifetime Withdrawal
9/12/2004	61	$200,000								
9/11/2005	61 - 62	$0	1.74 %	0.87 %	$201,744	$182,982	$178,938	4.36 %	$260,901	$0
9/11/2006	62 - 63	$0	2.98 %	1.48 %	$204,724	$189,392	$182,964	7.44 %	$280,309	$0
9/11/2007	63 - 64	$0	2.06 %	0.93 %	$206,619	$192,996	$187,080	5.14 %	$294,714	$0
9/11/2008	64 - 65	$0	4.86 %	2.45 %	$211,685	$199,705	$191,290	12.14 %	$330,507	$0
9/11/2009	65 - 66	$0	15.60 %	9.74 %	$232,304	$221,158	$195,594	38.99 %	$459,378	$0
9/11/2010	66 - 67	$0	6.75 %	3.69 %	$240,869	$231,593	$199,994	16.87 %	$536,861	$0
9/11/2011	67 - 68	$0	0.49 %	0.28 %	$241,547	$234,569	$204,494	1.21 %	$543,379	$0
9/11/2012	68 - 69	$0	12.39 %	5.67 %	$255,240	$250,300	$209,095	30.97 %	$711,654	$0
9/11/2013	69 - 70	$0	1.63 %	1.02 %	$257,833	$255,336	$213,800	4.08 %	$740,706	$0
9/11/2014	70 - 71	$0	45.07 %	26.56 %	$326,308	$326,308	$218,611	112.67 %	$1,575,287	$0
9/11/2015	71 - 72	$0	0.00 %	0.00 %	$259,358	$259,358	$155,073	0.00 %	$1,252,079	$66,950
9/11/2016	72 - 73	$0	2.30 %	2.29 %	$196,821	$196,821	$90,106	3.44 %	$960,866	$66,950
9/11/2017	73 - 74	$0	1.17 %	1.82 %	$129,886	$129,886	$21,322	1.76 %	$633,744	$69,253
9/11/2018	74 - 75	$0	14.01 %	12.83 %	$66,281	$66,281	$0	21.02 %	$346,872	$71,142
9/11/2019	75 - 76	$0	28.79 %	28.79 %	$0	$0	$0	43.19 %	$0	$84,943
9/11/2020	76 - 77	$0	5.16 %	5.16 %	$0	$0	$0	7.75 %	$0	$121,629
9/11/2021	77 - 78	$0	1.76 %	1.76 %	$0	$0	$0	2.63 %	$0	$131,052
9/11/2022	78 - 79	$0	1.36 %	1.36 %	$0	$0	$0	2.05 %	$0	$134,505
9/11/2023	79 - 80	$0	0.58 %	0.58 %	$0	$0	$0	0.87 %	$0	$137,256
		$200,000								$883,680

Well, you give up 50% of your account value growth. So, using the same hypothetical growth of 5% in one year, your account value would only grow by 2.5%. However, instead of your PIV income base growing by only 150% (7.5%), your income base would grow by 250% (12.5%).

That also grows the optional alternative death benefit if taken over a 5-year period (to a maximum of 250% of the account value) vs. a lump sum payout

If lifetime income is the main goal, then this product may be more appealing despite the slower growth of your account value and lump sum death benefit.

In the chart above, I've used the same 19-year period and the same combination of 1, 2, and 5-year indexes as in the previous chart. The same initial $200,000.

By focusing on the growth of the PIV columns with 250% (as opposed to 150%) while sacrificing 50% of the growth of the accumulation value, the income shown above starts out at over $66,000 rather than the $36,000 in the sister product.

The $66,000 starting income is based on a slightly lower joint payout factor (4.5%) but on a much larger PIV value ($1,575,000). The lowest guaranteed income is only $10,625 vs. $14,000 in its sister product (assuming every single year forever has a 0% interest credit).

The 250% PIV income growth stops when the lifetime income begins and reverts to only 150%, like its sister. In a written income plan, rather than use the $66,000 shown here, I'd conservatively use $40,000 or so, growing at the same average of 3%-4% over time.

Like its sister product, the death benefit works in the same manner. Should there be any funds left in the accumulation value column after the 2nd spouse passes away, then the beneficiaries each have the choice to take their share in a lump sum or over 5 years.

Since our accumulation value only grew by half as much since the focus was on PIV growth, the annuity runs out of money earlier than its sister, which means any residual death benefit for heirs disappears sooner.

But remember that income was the primary goal here. Again, every product, like everything else in this world, has pros and cons, positives and negatives. Nothing is perfect. We choose the product based on our needs and priorities.

There is also another possible benefit (for the first of these sister products only) – potential long-term care (LTC) benefits. Not only that policy (the 150% PIV grower, but also many GI policies work in a similar manner).

However, many insurance agents <u>oversell</u> this potential LTC benefit with these and similar products. I hardly bring it up because the moon and the stars must align to have it even apply or add value to your retirement planning.

But, should you or either of you in a joint lifetime income, need LTC, the income you are receiving will double for a period of no more than five years should you not be able to do 2 of the 6 Activities of Daily Living (eating, bathing, toileting, etc.)—<u>as long as there is money left in your account</u>.

And that's the rub. As you saw in the chart above since the income is so high, you run out of account value (but never run out of income) at about year 15. Well, that's earlier than most people may need LTC. Even if some money is left in the account, taking twice as much income out will cause it to run out even more quickly.

Once the account is depleted, the "doubler" stops, and the income returns to what it was prior to the need for LTC, and remains coming (and growing depending upon the GI bought) for as long as you or either of you lives.

So, please don't let some agent sell you on an LTC benefit because very few folks who want income will get any meaningful LTC benefits unless you have an LTC event very early in the income phase. This "potential" benefit is not a substitute for "real" long-term care insurance.

Having said that, here is one circumstance where it may be useful. Since there is no medical underwriting (no health questions), as these potential benefits are part of the GI contract, here is how I might position this policy.

If you are using funds to buy the GI that you do not need for income (whether it's non-qualified money or taking only RMDs from an IRA)—in other words, it's money you don't plan on spending—here's what I might suggest.

For the GI with the 150% income base grower, just never turn on the guaranteed income until your 80s or longer or until you need LTC. If it's an IRA, just take out the RMDs only (not the lifetime income) or take those RMDs from another IRA. Yes, you can do that.

That way, the income base will grow, even into your 80s or 90s. At some point, turn on the income base so you can reap the benefits of the GI, even if you never need LTC.

It's important to note this would not replace an LTC policy, but if your health, budget, or "use-it-or-lose-it" thinking doesn't allow you to buy LTC insurance, this idea is way better than nothing for funds you don't plan on spending.

Again, if we want to cut a piece of wood in 2, we use a saw, right? What is your primary goal for this particular money? Then, the decision and your confidence in that decision of which way to proceed become much easier.

As promised early in this chapter, I'd like to give you an example of a GI that is not performance-based. Although a performance-based GI may offer much higher potential income; with this GI, you know from the day you invest in it what your income will be. It's 100% guaranteed.

To compare against the last two GI examples, I'll use the same $200,000 investment, ages, and timing of the income. You'll notice the 0% returns every year and the payout factor of 8%. The guaranteed joint lifetime income is $28,347 per year. No doubts. 100% certain. A $200,000 bond fund cannot do that on a guaranteed basis.

This GI does have fees, and its surrender charge period is 12 years rather than the 10-year period for the other 2 GI examples (although the surrender charge period should be a non-issue if guaranteed lifetime income is the main purpose of this investment). It offers four 3-year indexes to choose from, and interest is only credited every 3 years.

With 0% returns every year (but with a bonus and an 8% roll-up), the guaranteed joint lifetime income of $28,347 is much higher than the performance-based GIs just described ($14,000 and $10,600).

		Earnings (blight) Percentage	Daily Account Value	Funwaal Value	Death Benefit	High Point Income Lifetime Death	Lifetime payout percentage	Withdrawals $ Dining	Cumulative Withdrawals
At issue		N/A	$200,000	$200,000	$180,000	$200,000	$260,000	0.00%		
1	61-62	0%	$200,000	$196,996	$178,678	$200,000	$280,000	4.45%		
2	62-63	0%	$200,000	$193,757	$175,722	$200,000	$303,204	4.52%		
3	63-64	0%	$200,000	$190,295	$180,278	$200,000	$327,525	4.61%		
4	64-65	0%	$200,000	$188,474	$181,595	$200,000	$353,727	4.68%		
5	65-66	0%	$200,000	$182,381	$182,644	$200,000	$382,025	4.60%		
6	66-67	0%	$200,000	$171,982	$183,393	$200,000	$412,587	4.69%		
7	67-68	0%	$200,000	$173,217	$183,507	$200,000	$445,594	4.74%		
8	68-69	0%	$200,000	$168,073	$183,847	$200,000	$481,241	4.80%		
9	69-70	0%	$200,000	$162,517	$183,473	$200,000	$519,740	4.88%		
10	70-71	0%	$200,000	$156,516	$182,039	$200,000	$561,326	4.94%		
11	71-72	0%	$200,000	$190,342	$181,604	$200,000	$561,325	5.05%		
12	72-73	0%	$115,821	$115,821	$151,758	$151,758	$561,320	5.05%	$28,347	$28,347
13	73-74	0%	$81,300	$81,300	$121,060	$121,060	$561,320	5.05%	$28,347	$56,694
14	74-75	0%	$40,779	$40,779	$89,486	$89,486	$561,320	5.05%	$28,347	$85,041
15	75-76	0%	$12,258	$12,258	$57,017	$57,017	$561,320	5.05%	$28,347	$113,388
16	76-77	0%	$0	$0	$0	$0	$561,320	5.05%	$28,347	$141,735
17	77-78	0%	$0	$0	$0	$0	$561,320	5.05%	$28,347	$170,082
18	78-79	0%	$0	$0	$0	$0	$561,320	5.05%	$28,347	$198,429
19	79-80	0%	$0	$0	$0	$0	$561,320	5.05%	$28,347	$226,776
20	80-81	0%	$0	$0	$0	$0	$561,320	5.05%	$28,347	$255,123
21	81-82	0%	$0	$0	$0	$0	$561,320	5.05%	$28,347	$283,470
22	82-83	0%	$0	$0	$0	$0	$561,320	5.05%	$28,347	$311,817
23	83-84	0%	$0	$0	$0	$0	$561,320	5.05%	$28,347	$340,164
24	84-85	0%	$0	$0	$0	$0	$561,320	5.05%	$28,347	$368,511
25	85-86	0%	$0	$0	$0	$0	$561,320	5.05%	$28,347	$396,858
26	86-87	0%	$0	$0	$0	$0	$561,320	5.05%	$28,347	$425,205
27	87-88	0%	$0	$0	$0	$0	$561,320	5.05%	$28,347	$453,552
28	88-89	0%	$0	$0	$0	$0	$561,320	5.05%	$28,347	$481,899
29	89-90	0%	$0	$0	$0	$0	$561,320	5.05%	$28,347	$510,246
30	90-91	0%	$0	$0	$0	$0	$561,320	5.05%	$28,347	$538,593

Guaranteed contract minimum (assumed 0%) illustration table

This is one hypothetical outcome of the product's performance and not a guarantee of future results. Please review all hypothetical scenarios included.

Not shown in this chart is the hypothetical income based on backcasting the index returns. Using those returns, the initial income is $65,000/year, which might increase. That's about the same as the second GI and has a higher potential than its sister ($50,000) per year. Also, this GI has no LTC provisions at all. Not a deal killer.

So far, we have discussed BUFFERs and accumulation-only FIAs and GIs that offer something no other product but an annuity can - a guaranteed lifetime income. Which broad type is better? Of course, that depends on what your primary goal for this portion of your money is.

Before I introduce a few FIAs with a unique benefit from most others, I want to bring in the "brother" annuity to the two sisters covered over the last several pages. It's an

FIA that my wife Norma has added to her retirement portfolio from a partial in-service 401(k) rollover.

Technically, it is a GI but without an income base (a phantom value like PIV). There are only two account values: the accumulation value and the surrender value.

It has the accumulation properties of a BUFFER (with a mandatory fee) plus an optional lifetime income based on the account value, which makes it an interesting choice.

Like its sisters, it has the same indexes, although it has no potential LTC benefits (which is normally NOT a reason to purchase an FIA). It also comes with a mandatory fee, which does two things.

Number 1, prior to turning on your lifetime income (which could be never if you treat it like a BUFFER), whatever the indexes earn, they actually credit your cash account with 5% more. If an index earns 10%, your accumulation value will grow by 10.5%. Again, there is no phantom income base as there is with GIs. That cash is all yours after the 10-year surrender period if you want it.

The other benefit of having that fee is an escalating payout factor, which is calculated by how long you delay turning on the lifetime income as well as the age of the younger joint spouse. This payout factor will usually be much higher than its sisters and most other GIs.

Although, again, no product is perfect, this one gives you

the safe (no market risk) accumulation potential that you desire while also offering an attractive lifetime income should you ever decide to turn it on. Flexibility for sure.

You'll notice the accumulation in the hypothetical client illustration in the next image is much greater than in its sisters, but the income turned on in the same year is similar to the 2nd GI discussed. The death benefit is only the accumulation value—while it lasts.

Example: Hypothetical Values Over the Last 19 Years for a contract issued on 9/12/2004

Contract Year	Age	Net Premiums[1]	End of Year Credited Interest Rate[2]	End of Year Accumulation Value	End of Year Pre-MVA Cash Surrender Value[6]	End of Year Guaranteed Minimum Value[3]	Lifetime Withdrawal Percent	360 Benefit Annual Income Withdrawal	Death Benefit
9/12/2004	61	$200,000							
9/11/2005	61 - 62	$0	1.89 %	$201,849	$181,664	$177,014	5.30 %	$0	$201,849
9/11/2006	62 - 63	$0	3.13 %	$206,188	$185,569	$179,056	5.75 %	$0	$206,188
9/11/2007	63 - 64	$0	2.13 %	$208,569	$190,319	$181,103	6.20 %	$0	$208,569
9/11/2008	64 - 65	$0	5.04 %	$216,999	$200,724	$183,172	6.65 %	$0	$216,999
9/11/2009	65 - 66	$0	21.36 %	$260,838	$244,535	$185,207	7.10 %	$0	$260,838
9/11/2010	66 - 67	$0	7.24 %	$277,058	$263,205	$186,866	7.55 %	$0	$277,058
9/11/2011	67 - 68	$0	0.55 %	$275,942	$265,594	$188,406	8.00 %	$0	$275,942
9/11/2012	68 - 69	$0	11.85 %	$305,700	$298,057	$189,992	8.45 %	$0	$305,700
9/11/2013	69 - 70	$0	2.14 %	$309,275	$305,409	$191,328	8.90 %	$0	$309,275
9/11/2014	70 - 71	$0	59.21 %	$487,734	$487,734	$192,659	9.35 %	$0	$487,734
9/11/2015	71 - 72	$0	0.00 %	$435,303	$435,303	$143,430	9.80 %	$47,798	$435,303
9/11/2016	72 - 73	$0	2.07 %	$391,305	$391,305	$93,599	0.00 %	$47,798	$391,305
9/11/2017	73 - 74	$0	1.55 %	$344,040	$344,040	$42,057	0.00 %	$48,787	$344,040
9/11/2018	74 - 75	$0	11.89 %	$325,863	$325,863	$0	0.00 %	$49,542	$325,863
9/11/2019	75 - 76	$0	38.54 %	$370,353	$370,353	$0	0.00 %	$55,433	$370,353
9/11/2020	76 - 77	$0	4.63 %	$303,478	$303,478	$0	0.00 %	$76,795	$303,478
9/11/2021	77 - 78	$0	1.64 %	$223,864	$223,864	$0	0.00 %	$80,353	$223,864
9/11/2022	78 - 79	$0	1.25 %	$141,809	$141,809	$0	0.00 %	$81,675	$141,809
9/11/2023	79 - 80	$0	0.49 %	$58,049	$58,049	$0	0.00 %	$82,694	$58,049
		$200,000						$570,875	

The 4th column, "interest credited," includes the 5% bonus to your account value until (and if) the lifetime income is started. Then, the account only grows by what the indexes earn.

Same with the lifetime income. It grows each year by what the indexes earn (not 150% as in its sisters). So, you do give up faster potential income (PIV) growth for the larger accumulation potential.

The interesting thing to note on the chart is the growing (until the income is turned on) joint lifetime payout factor of 9.8%. It's way higher than the 4%-5% of its sisters at the same age. The starting income shown in the chart is $47,000, so it's similar to the younger sister GI discussed.

The worst-case guaranteed income is $19,600 for a joint lifetime income, which is much higher than the others.

Let's revisit the 4% rule, which has no joint lifetime income guarantees (only the hope of a 30-year retirement). Even the worst-case guaranteed income, which assumes ZERO returns for every year for the rest of both lives, you would need an investment of $490,000 to provide that "hope."

That's 245% more money needed to provide the same amount of non-guaranteed income. But let's say that this accumulation FIA's indexes only earns 3% net of fees. Keep in mind the 5% bonus to the account value of whatever the indexes earn until the lifetime income is started.

That would make the account value $247,000 when the income is turned on. At a 9.8% payout factor, the joint lifetime income would start out at $24,294.

Using the 4% rule again, you would need $607,425 to provide that level of non-guaranteed income for a "hoped-for" 30-year retirement. But using these very conservative assumptions, we did it with $200,000 with no market risk.

The death benefit is noted in the far-right column. As with

its sisters, the income is so high in relation to the account value (with an initial 9.8% payout factor) that eventually (about year 20), there is no cash left in the policy—only lifetime income for as long as the last spouse lives.

You may well be thinking, how can an insurance company pay an increasing income when there is no money left in the account? Your 401(k) cannot do that.

All annuity income guarantees (including SPIAs) operate on the basis of math and actuarial science. It's actuarial science that academic researchers refer to as "mortality credits."

And no type of investment, other than insurance, can provide mortality credits. It's the mathematical science of risk-pooling. Actuaries, who are the "rocket scientists" of the insurance world, do that math very well.

If you own life insurance, you already have mortality credits working on your behalf. How else can a life insurance company pay a $1,000,000 death benefit on a 27-year-old male with a 30-year term policy who had only made two $35 monthly premiums and then got killed by a drunk driver?

The insurer knows that most 27-year-olds will live for many decades and outlive the 30-year term and scientifically priced this into the required premiums.

Actuarial science allows the insurance company to pay

that death benefit because they know exactly how many 27-year-old males will die in any year. They don't know which ones will die or how, but they know how many will. That's actuarial science.

On the opposite side of that science is how long 71-year-old females will live and be paid a continuing income from an annuity. They don't know which ones will pass away, but going forward, they know how many each year will. It's just science based on decades of actual experience.

By leveraging mortality credits, income annuities can provide amazing "retirement income alpha." Only insurance companies can manufacture high cash flow that is totally uncorrelated to the volatile markets and perfectly hedges the risk of living too long. You cannot get these valuable mortality credits anywhere else.

Insurance companies work both sides of the coin (actuarial science) to their benefit. The risk to the insurer of a life insurance policy is the policyholder dying too soon. The risk to the insurer of an annuity is someone living way too long. If they lose on one side, they gain on the other side.

Whether it is life insurance premiums or annuities guaranteed income, the insurance company pools tens of thousands of lives to reduce their risk and offer the lowest life insurance premiums and highest annuity income payouts possible and still produce a nice profit.

Here's something to think about. Many folks ask me,

"What is the internal rate of return on a guaranteed income annuity?" I answer by saying, "What do you want it to be?" The truth is the insurance company does NOT set that rate of return alone. No, they don't.

You see, YOU (and perhaps your spouse) determine what the true internal rate of return will be—by how long one or both of you will live. The longer one lives, the better. That's mortality credits providing guaranteed retirement income alpha that you cannot get anywhere else.

Mortality credits are based on a person's age and gender. If you and/or your spouse are very healthy, well-educated, and take care of yourselves, the likelihood is that one/both of you will live much longer than the average person's life expectancy. To get an even better return, just live longer!

And enjoy the insurance company's money for a change.

Would you like to get a "scientific" estimate on how long you will probably live based on your answers to questions about your health, family history, lifestyle, education, and background?

There are a number of these sites, but the one that I used was: www.livingto100.com.

Here's an example of guaranteed mortality credits working for a couple. Scott and Diane (both age 56) wanted to know how much they would have to invest to get a GUARANTEED joint lifetime income of $3,000/month

($36,000/yr.) when they retired at age 67 to supplement their Social Security checks and his federal pension.

And they wanted that income to be guaranteed with 0% returns every year during that 10-year waiting period.

The actuaries came back with a figure of $492,301. Yes, that exact figure is based on their ages and when they wanted to begin their joint lifetime income.

Let's revisit the 4% rule (non-guaranteed) again. What income would the 4% rule suggest on that $492,301 investment? Well, it's only $1,641/ month ($19,692/year). And there's no guarantee that where they invest their money in the ten years prior to retirement won't lose money by then.

Would you rather have a <u>guaranteed</u> $3,000/month... or a 4% rule-inspired, subject-to-market-risk, monthly income of $1,641? But wait, there's more. At an average inflation rate of 3%, it would take 21 years in retirement for that $1,641/month to grow to the same guaranteed $3,000/month they've enjoyed all along. Although it's not guaranteed, the initial $3,000 income should grow even higher during those 21 years. They'll be 88 years old then!

Let's look at this same situation in another way. That $492,301 invested in the GI equals a $900,000 investment in the market using the 4% rule since 4% of $900,000 is $36,000. What if you haven't saved $900,000 yet?

Now, to be fair, stock market-based investments do have more upside potential. But along with the larger potential comes risk—substantial risks in the "retirement red zone."

What if Scott and Diane only had $500,000 in savings and didn't want to take risks being only ten years from retirement? Well, the 4% rule ($20,000) certainly wouldn't work for them as to their income goal or to eliminate longevity risk since it provides only 55% of the $36,000 income that's absolutely guaranteed in the GI.

And the income from the GI should be even greater than $3,000 since it's unlikely that the indexes will earn nothing for ten years. That's the worst-case scenario, not the best-case or even the most likely case.

And the income will last beyond age 100 if needed as opposed to the 4% rule's "hoped-for" 30 years.

This example shows how $492,301 invested in an FIA now can most likely equal the heavy "income-lifting" of $900,000 by using actuarial science and mortality credits.

You see, in the "probability-based" mindset using "asset allocation," one needs 100% of their money invested at all times in order to make the 4% withdrawal rate work with a 90% probability of not running out of money over 30 years.

The GI is guaranteed to never run out or stop coming in as long as either one lives.

That's mortality credits at work. Something no mutual funds, ETFs, bank accounts, hedge funds, or private equity can offer. Again, no place to invest your money is perfect. Know what's important to you, and then make a plan.

But let's say their GI doesn't earn zeros for the first ten years. The illustration, using historical backcasting, shows an income of $6,000/month. So there is a big upside with this particular product to the guaranteed level of income!

Now, this particular GI product has a higher "guaranteed" incomes than most others (with 0% returns), but once you turn on the guaranteed income, whether it was the $3,000 figure based on 0% returns or the $6,000 monthly figure, it usually stays pretty level for the rest of your life.

But I'll put the guarantees of this GI from a household name insurer against the 4% rule, any day of the week.

What's more important to you? Higher guarantees or higher potential initial income with annual raises based on what the indexes earn every year during your retirement? There's no wrong answer. It's purely a matter of personal preferences.

This book is simply trying to expand your financial options.

Special Situation FIAs Worth Knowing About

Dana and her husband feel most comfortable always having $350,000 to $400,000 in cash for emergencies.

I believed that given their personal circumstances, that was too much money earning virtually nothing in the bank.

I asked if they would consider adding another $100,000 FIA investment to the $300,000 BUFFER they had already agreed to as part of my RMD withdrawal strategy. That would still leave them with $250,000+ in cash emergency funds.

This is one of the ideas that I presented to them. It's not a GI, but kind of like a "Swiss army knife" BUFFER.

Again, I told them that the next 10-20 years likely won't be as good as the last, so like all the other illustrations in this book, don't be dazzled by the returns shown. Let's cut them in half. Certainly, they'll be better than what the bank was paying them.

This particular product adds 15% of actual cash to whatever is deposited, so the $100,000 accumulation value is increased by $15,000. That's much better than the toaster oven I was given to open a bank account when I was a teenager!

However, that cash bonus does have a 10-year vesting period.

Like the other FIAs, there are one-year and 2-year indexes, which is why you see the larger backcasted returns in the even years. No withdrawals are planned until one of 3 things might happen.

NON-GUARANTEED ANNUITY CONTRACT VALUES
MOST RECENT PERIOD from 12/31/2011 to 12/31/2021

This chart illustrates total contract values based on the ten most recent years of historical index performance, current Rider Charge, selected withdrawals, the initial allocation, current Strategy Charges and current rates. The Accumulation Value reflects applicable Rider Charges and Strategy Charges.

	10 Years	20 Years
Annual Effective Rate	13.29%	12.97%
Net Annual Effective Rate	11.08%	10.77%

End of Year	Covered Person Start Age/End Age	Net Term Credited Rate	Accumulation Value	Annual Withdrawals [1] (Beginning of Year)	Surrender Value [2]	Living Benefit Base (ADL Benefit/Plan Gap® Benefit) [3]	Death Benefit [4]	Enhanced Death Benefit [5]
At Issue	61		$115,000			$115,000		$115,000
1	61 / 62	0.62%	$115,709	$0	$89,948	$116,419	$119,746	$124,491
2	62 / 63	13.22%	$131,003	$0	$105,319	$147,005	$138,738	$162,476
3	63 / 64	6.76%	$139,852	$0	$114,846	$164,704	$160,600	$206,200
4	64 / 65	10.66%	$154,766	$0	$129,873	$194,532	$169,395	$223,790
5	65 / 66	7.03%	$165,644	$0	$141,239	$216,288	$182,895	$250,790
6	66 / 67	21.19%	$200,738	$0	$176,436	$286,475	$223,196	$331,391
7	67 / 68	3.89%	$208,555	$0	$187,039	$302,111	$222,118	$329,236
8	68 / 69	12.72%	$235,083	$0	$215,279	$355,165	$260,315	$405,629
9	69 / 70	9.54%	$257,499	$0	$240,131	$399,999	$303,156	$491,312
10	70 / 71	27.71%	$328,852	$0	$328,852	$542,704	$328,852	$542,704
11	71 / 72	-0.75%	$326,391	$0	$326,391	$537,782	$343,887	$572,774
12	72 / 73	27.49%	$416,101	$0	$416,101	$717,202	$416,101	$717,202
13	73 / 74	0.15%	$416,714	$0	$416,714	$718,428	$460,683	$806,367
14	74 / 75	19.72%	$498,885	$0	$498,885	$882,769	$498,885	$882,769
15	75 / 76	-0.99%	$493,970	$0	$493,970	$872,941	$519,652	$924,303
16	76 / 77	33.27%	$658,296	$0	$658,296	$1,201,592	$658,296	$1,201,592
17	77 / 78	-1.95%	$645,459	$0	$645,459	$1,175,919	$645,459	$1,175,919
18	78 / 79	14.91%	$741,715	$0	$741,715	$1,368,431	$741,715	$1,368,431
19	79 / 80	-0.49%	$738,053	$0	$738,053	$1,361,106	$810,275	$1,505,549
20	80 / 81	20.43%	$888,836	$0	$888,836	$1,662,672	$888,836	$1,662,672
30	90 / 91	21.35 %	$2,454,069	$0	$2,454,069	$1,662,672	$2,454,069	$1,662,672
54	114 / 115	26.44 %	$31,135,737	$0	$31,135,737	$1,662,672	$31,135,737	$1,662,672

In the 4th column, you can see the accumulation value growing. And the 5th column is the surrender values. They look very much like the BUFFERs I use in my practice.

But the 6th column is the heart of this "Swiss army knife." It's the "Living Benefit Base," and its value can only be used in one of 3 ways. These values grow at 200% of what the indexes do (minus fees). And this living benefit base grows at this rate for only 15-20 years, based on one's age.

The chart shows that at Dana's age of 80, the cash value is some $888,000, and the Benefit Base is $1,600,000. Again, let's cut all these figures in half, OK?

In the illustration, at age 75, her living benefit base is about $882,000. Assuming that was so, here are the three ways that Dana could take advantage of the benefit base.

Let's say at age 75, Dana needs LTC (needing help in 2 of the 6 Activities of Daily Living (ADLs). She could opt to take whatever the benefit base was ($882,769) and use it to pay for care in her home, an assisted living facility, or a nursing home over seven years or $126,110/year.

Unfortunately, this LTC-like benefit (like many FIAs) does not cover Alzheimer's or any form of dementia—it would only kick in if 2 ADL triggers were met.

Now, it's more likely that she would need LTC closer to age 80 than age 75. In that case, the benefit base shown then is $1.6 million, not the pictured $882,769 below.

Activities of Daily Living (ADL) Benefit
The Activities of Daily Living (ADL) Benefit can be triggered if the covered person cannot perform two of the six activities of daily living for 90 days with the expectation of permanence. The owner can receive the ADL Benefit even if the covered person is not confined. The six activities of daily life include: bathing, continence, dressing, eating, toileting, and transferring. The ADL Benefit is equal to the Benefit Base paid out in 7 equal annual payments.

$882,769 Age 75 → $126,110 7 Year Pay

Upon qualification for the ADL benefit, the client can elect to receive seven equal payments of the Benefit Base.

But let's cut that by 60% if the FIA doesn't perform anywhere near as shown because I don't think the next decade will be as good as the last. If I'm wrong, so be it. Either way, the policy will be a wonderful bond alternative.

That figure would still be an attractive $640,000 (or $91,000 for seven years) at her age of 80. That would go a long way to the cost of care twenty years from now. That would end her policy when those seven years were over.

Anyway, if Dana didn't live for all those seven years, the remainder would be paid out annually to her beneficiaries. This benefit does not replace LTC insurance, just as I've written previously about other FIAs. But it is one way to take advantage of the benefit base with no medical questions whatsoever. No health underwriting at all.

The next way Dana might use the benefit base is if Social Security reduces everyone's benefits by 3% or more.

We've all seen the note on our Social Security statement that says unless Congress does something, in 2033 or thereabouts, they'll only have enough revenue to pay

80% of your promised benefits. That's a 20% potential cut and way more than the 3% needed to trigger this benefit.

So if Congress reduces your benefit by means-testing or any other similar cut (paying higher Medicare premiums due to the IRRMA tables being specifically excluded) that's applied to Americans, then Dana might opt to use her benefit base for this contingency to try and make up for losses to her Social Security check.

Her benefit base in 2032 is $542,000. If Social Security cuts her benefits, say by means-testing, she could take that benefit base over 12 years and get an extra $45,000/year to help offset those reduced Social Security checks.

Let's cut that by 60%, and she would still get $18,000/year, which may be more than the 20% loss from Social Security.

If Dana didn't live for those dozen years, the balance of payments would go to her beneficiaries.

PlanGap Benefit

The PlanGap® Benefit can be elected if the Income Gap Benefit Index is reduced by more than 3%¹. The PlanGap® Benefit is equal to the Benefit Base paid out in 12 equal annual payments. The PlanGap® Benefit is not a replacement for social security benefits but provides a benefit designed to mitigate a reduction.

Year	2032	2033	2034	2035	2036	2037	2038	2039	2040	2041	2042	2043
Age	71	72	73	74	75	76	77	78	79	80	81	82
Income	$45,225	$45,225	$45,225	$45,225	$45,225	$45,225	$45,225	$45,225	$45,225	$45,225	$45,225	$45,225

$542,704 Total PlanGap® Benefit

The 3rd potential way to use this FIA is by your beneficiaries deciding to take the death benefit over 5 years rather than taking a lump sum.

If you were a beneficiary, wouldn't you want the option to get over $200,000 more, as in this example?

Income taxes might drive that decision, as getting a lump sum of $328,000 would push many beneficiaries into the highest marginal tax bracket. In that case, spreading a 65% larger benefit out over 5 years might make more sense.

Offer loved ones their choice of death benefit

An Interesting Life Insurance Alternative for IRAs

Here's an example of another unique FIA that does what most others do not. Too few agents understand how to take advantage of a powerful provision in the contract other than using it as a guaranteed lifetime income (GI) annuity. But check this out.

Just yesterday, I did this illustration for a client aged 65 who wanted to retire ASAP. I designed a written retirement income plan (called my retirement income roadmap) for her, and she was going to be fine through age 100, even with my typically conservative assumptions.

Valerie was primarily concerned with her own retirement, but if there could be a legacy for her son, in addition to her home, which will be paid off in a few years, that would be even better.

She had a TSP (the 401K-like plan for federal employees), which had $625,000, which she would never need for income due to her large pension, Social Security, rental property, and other savings. She decided to use $500,000 from her TSP to fund this account.

This FIA has a very attractive rider that offers guaranteed legacy growth – even with taking Required Minimum Distributions (RMDs)

Look at how the death benefit grows over time – even though she'll have to take RMDs from age 73 and beyond.

The chart below shows the GUARANTEED benefits of this annuity. This chart depicts the worst-case scenario of the indexes earning ZERO every year. Any gains the indexes have will increase both the RMDs and the death benefit.

She doesn't want or need the income, but the IRS makes her take those pesky RMD withdrawals in the 4th column.

Just look at the second column from the right, which

shows a growing death benefit (taxable since this is an IRA). The accumulation value comes with an immediate 13% cash bonus, while the death benefit is growing by a guaranteed 5% until she begins taking the RMDs (for up to 20 years). At that time, the RMD withdrawals offset the 5% growth in the death benefit on a dollar-for-dollar basis.

Here's a view of Guaranteed Annuity Contract Values
Annual Assumed Interest Rate: 0.00%

The Assumed Interest Rate does not reflect charges. However, charges are reflected in the Accumulation Value.

This hypothetical illustration is based on the allocation percentages and rates that are current as of the Assumed Issue Date of this illustration. This hypothetical illustration is based on a $500,000 Premium Amount.

| Year Ending | Beginning of Year Age | End of Year Age | RMD Withdrawals¹ | Base Contract Values | | | | Family Endowment Rider Death Benefit³ ($5.00%) | Cumulative Withdrawals |
				Minimum Guaranteed Contract Value	Cash Surrender Value²	Accumulation Value	Base Death Benefit²		
11/2024	65	66	$0	$442,172	$442,172	$560,750	$565,000	$525,000	$0
11/2025	66	67	$0	$446,724	$446,724	$556,288	$565,000	$551,250	$0
11/2026	67	68	$0	$451,145	$451,145	$551,602	$565,000	$578,813	$0
11/2027	68	69	$0	$455,419	$455,419	$546,682	$565,000	$607,753	$0
11/2028	69	70	$0	$459,532	$459,532	$541,516	$565,000	$638,141	$0
11/2029	70	71	$0	$463,468	$463,468	$536,092	$565,000	$670,048	$0
11/2030	71	72	$0	$467,211	$467,211	$530,396	$565,000	$703,550	$0
11/2031	72	73	$0	$470,742	$470,742	$524,416	$565,000	$738,728	$0
11/2032	73	74	$19,789	$454,254	$454,254	$498,348	$545,211	$755,875	$19,789
11/2033	74	75	$19,543	$437,527	$437,527	$472,380	$525,668	$774,126	$39,332
11/2034	75	76	$19,202	$420,641	$420,641	$446,597	$506,465	$793,629	$58,535
11/2035	76	77	$18,844	$403,600	$403,600	$421,008	$487,621	$814,467	$77,379
11/2036	77	78	$22,062	$382,813	$476,225	$476,225	$476,225	$832,373	$99,440
11/2037	78	79	$21,647	$361,860	$447,503	$447,503	$447,503	$852,345	$121,087
11/2038	79	80	$21,209	$340,745	$422,705	$419,049	$422,705	$873,753	$142,295
11/2039	80	81	$20,926	$319,295	$401,779	$390,697	$401,779	$896,515	$163,221
11/2040	81	82	$20,710	$297,426	$381,068	$362,366	$381,068	$918,825	$183,932
11/2041	82	83	$20,598	$275,028	$360,470	$333,958	$360,470	$939,670	$204,530
11/2042	83	84	$20,366	$252,225	$340,105	$305,605	$340,105	$958,453	$224,895
11/2043	84	85	$20,244	$228,914	$319,860	$277,214	$319,860	$973,660	$245,140
11/2044	85	86	$19,991	$213,616	$299,869	$257,222	$299,869	$937,456	$265,131
11/2045	86	87	$19,728	$198,266	$280,141	$237,494	$280,141	$898,612	$284,859
11/2046	87	88	$19,454	$182,877	$260,687	$218,040	$260,687	$856,948	$304,313
11/2047	88	89	$19,028	$167,597	$241,658	$199,012	$241,658	$812,855	$323,342
11/2048	89	90	$18,733	$152,300	$222,925	$180,279	$222,925	$765,606	$342,075
11/2049	90	91	$18,273	$137,150	$204,653	$162,006	$204,653	$715,691	$360,347
11/2050	91	92	$17,796	$122,165	$186,857	$144,210	$186,857	$663,014	$378,143

Even with no earnings whatsoever, at age 92, she will have taken out $378,143 of total RMDs (far right column), and there will still be a $663,014 death benefit. That is a combined total of over $1,041,000 at 0% earnings!

But annuities do not earn nothing for 30 years. What if this FIA only averaged 4%? What would the RMD income and death benefit look like?

Well, the next chart shows this. The RMDs start at over $27,000 and grow to over $40,000 over time.

But look at the death benefit column (2nd from the right). It shows the cumulative RMDs taken by age 92 to be some $600,000 and the remaining death benefit of $581,000. That's a combined total of $1,181,000 with no stock market risk.

Year Ending	Beginning of Year Age	End of Year Age	RMD Withdrawals	Cash Surrender Value	Accumulation Value	Balanced Allocation Value	Base Death Benefit	Family Endowment Rider Death Benefit (5.00%)	Cumulative Withdrawals
11/2024	65	66	$0	$442,172	$560,750	$583,180	$583,180	$525,000	$0
11/2025	66	67	$0	$471,315	$601,681	$601,631	$601,681	$551,250	$0
11/2026	67	68	$0	$472,873	$596,995	$620,875	$620,875	$578,813	$0
11/2027	68	69	$0	$506,779	$640,388	$640,388	$640,388	$607,753	$0
11/2028	69	70	$0	$510,773	$635,222	$660,631	$660,631	$638,141	$0
11/2029	70	71	$0	$550,004	$681,190	$681,190	$681,190	$670,048	$0
11/2030	71	72	$0	$553,956	$675,474	$702,514	$702,514	$703,550	$0
11/2031	72	73	$0	$596,313	$724,147	$724,147	$724,147	$738,728	$0
11/2032	73	74	$27,326	$572,857	$691,592	$719,256	$719,256	$748,338	$27,326
11/2033	74	75	$27,121	$595,089	$714,025	$714,025	$714,025	$758,633	$54,448
11/2034	75	76	$29,025	$573,668	$679,667	$706,854	$706,854	$767,540	$83,473
11/2035	76	77	$28,678	$600,086	$699,394	$699,394	$699,394	$777,239	$112,151
11/2036	77	78	$30,541	$664,936	$663,421	$689,958	$689,958	$785,559	$142,692
11/2037	78	79	$30,224	$680,109	$680,109	$680,109	$680,109	$794,613	$172,916
11/2038	79	80	$32,233	$643,738	$642,362	$668,057	$668,057	$802,111	$205,149
11/2039	80	81	$31,868	$655,537	$655,537	$655,537	$655,537	$810,348	$237,017
11/2040	81	82	$33,791	$617,379	$616,158	$640,804	$640,804	$816,797	$270,808
11/2041	82	83	$33,372	$625,555	$625,555	$625,555	$625,555	$823,454	$304,180
11/2042	83	84	$35,342	$585,619	$584,573	$607,956	$607,956	$827,814	$339,522
11/2043	84	85	$34,858	$589,805	$589,805	$589,805	$589,805	$832,035	$374,380
11/2044	85	86	$36,863	$555,211	$554,360	$576,534	$576,534	$792,411	$411,243
11/2045	86	87	$36,527	$563,069	$563,069	$563,069	$563,069	$752,914	$447,770
11/2046	87	88	$39,102	$526,132	$525,471	$546,490	$546,490	$710,526	$486,872
11/2047	88	89	$38,404	$529,945	$529,945	$529,945	$529,945	$668,941	$525,276
11/2048	89	90	$41,081	$490,903	$490,444	$510,062	$510,062	$624,585	$566,357
11/2049	90	91	$40,238	$490,227	$490,227	$490,227	$490,227	$581,424	$606,595

I also ran the same using actual calendar returns of the last ten years of the S&P 500 index with a 0% floor and a 64% participation rate in the index's return (repeated 3 times).

That illustration shows the RMDs growing from $38,000 to $91,000 at age 92, with a remaining death benefit of $1.1 million. The combined death benefit and RMD income totals over $2.2 million.

Sounds a little like a life insurance policy in some respects (but taxable), and with zero medical underwriting needed. No health questions and no exams.

A True Long-Term Care (LTC) Annuity

There are a few annuities that have no real purpose other than to be an alternative to those who plan on self-funding potential future LTC expenses. They don't offer much in the way of accumulation and no lifetime income benefits. They only offer a residual death benefit of the account value should no long-term care payouts ever occur.

Unlike some of the FIAs described earlier that "might" offer some LTC benefits, these products do have at least some medical underwriting. One can get turned down.

John and Shannon are a 65-year-old couple who fully understand the likelihood of one or both needing years of expensive long-term care down the road. So, they decided to invest $150,000 into an LTC annuity. They used funds from what's called a 1035 tax-free exchange of an expensive variable annuity they no longer wanted but they could have used funds from any type of account.

If one or both need care and qualify for benefits, they EACH could get $3,365/month for up to 30 months. That initial benefit has no inflation protection. But should either of them need more months of care, that $3,365 increases by 5% per year (after the 30 months of care) and would be for <u>unlimited</u> years beyond those 30 months.

So, at age 85, EACH could get up to $110,000/year in TAX-FREE LTC benefits for many years at home or anywhere. That's a game-changer from a $150,000 investment!

The Death of a Spouse in Retirement

Not a cheery topic by any means. But it's one that, as a retirement income planner, I must deal with almost every single year. On every level, this is a tough assignment.

Besides the obvious, I'll focus on just income taxes and Medicare Part B and D premiums after a spouse dies. It's not pretty.

In 2020, let's say that a 72-year-old couple was enjoying a modified AGI of $181,000. We'll ignore any potential state/local income taxes for this example.

Let's suppose the husband died in 2021 and in 2022 she is filing as a single taxpayer. Let's look at her taxes.

Rate	For Unmarried Individuals	For Married Individuals Filing Joint Returns	For Heads of Households
10%	$0 to $10,275	$0 to $20,550	$0 to $14,650
12%	$10,275 to $41,775	$20,550 to $83,550	$14,650 to $55,900
22%	$41,775 to $89,075	$83,550 to $178,150	$55,900 to $89,050
24%	$89,075 to $170,050	$178,150 to $340,100	$89,050 to $170,050
32%	$170,050 to $215,950	$340,100 to $431,900	$170,050 to $215,950
35%	$215,950 to $539,900	$431,900 to $647,850	$215,950 to $539,900
37%	$539,900 or more	$647,850 or more	$539,900 or more

Source: Internal Revenue Service

She inherited her late husband's IRA and kept their joint lifetime guaranteed income (GI) annuity, so the RMDs and other taxable income would be the same.

Of course, her Social Security income would decrease as she would keep the larger check and lose the smaller Social Security check (it matters not which spouse passes).

With the reduced Social Security income, her modified AGI would be $171,000 (2022). But her standard deduction would only be $14,350 instead of the joint deduction of $28,700. That leaves her paying income taxes on $156,650, which would be about $31,263.

That's more than $6,500 higher than what they would have paid should he still be alive! But it gets worse.

In my other books, I've written about the IRMAA tables, which determine if a couple or person would pay a <u>surcharge</u> on their Medicare Part B & D premiums or not.

Individual MAGI	Couples MAGI	Part B Surcharge	Part D Surcharge
< $88,000	< $176,000	No surcharge	No surcharge
$88,000 - $111,000	$176,000 - $222,000	$59.40 a month	$12.30 a month
$111,000 - $138,000	$222,000 - $276,000	$148.50 a month	#31.80 a month
$138,000 - $165,000	$276,000 - $330,000	$237.60 a month	$51.20 a month
$165,000 - $500,000	$330,000 - $750,000	$326.70 a month	$70.70 a month
$500,000 and greater	$750,000 and greater	$356.40 a month	$77.10 a month

Now, in reality, there is a 2-year delay in assessing income for IRMAA purposes. For example, 2022 Medicare premiums are determined by income in 2020. But let's leave that aside for now and look at the bigger picture.

As a couple, in 2022, they each would pay an extra $180.30 monthly for Parts B & D ($2,163.60/yr. each).

But as a single filer, her penalty is $288.80 per month ON TOP OF the regular $170.10 due to her income. That's a total premium surcharge of $3,465.60 per year). That's an extra $1,302 penalty... just for being a widow(er)!

OK, there's the potential problem. What are my solutions?

Well, those who have done retirement income plans with me know that I am a big advocate of ROTH conversions using tax bracket management. What this couple should have done is do ROTH conversions all along—especially before RMDs must begin at age 73. Proactive tax planning.

I also recommend to most folks that they contribute to a ROTH instead of a traditional (deductible) IRA.

There are no RMDs on ROTHs, and more importantly, income from ROTHS is NOT taxable. Nor does ROTH income figure into the IRMAA calculations to determine Medicare premiums. A ROTH would completely change her tax situation for the better.

Why doesn't everyone contribute to a ROTH or convert their IRAs to ROTHs? Because they don't like paying taxes. But taxes are going to be due some time. There's no escaping them. That's the deal you signed up for with the IRS when you took the tax deductions for your IRA contributions. They are a "not-so-silent" partner.

I'd much rather pay taxes at known rates, brackets, and deductions today than at unknown rates, brackets, and deductions in the future. The taxes are owed to the IRS. I'd rather pay them on my terms than leave it to theirs.

Whether you use IRAs at Fidelity or Schwab or IRAs invested in any of the fixed indexed annuities described herein, please consider ROTHs as part of your planning process.

Ruling from the Grave - Stretching an Inheritance

You may have heard about the Stretch IRA, which allows non-spousal beneficiaries to stretch their inherited IRA over their lifetime. By stretching an IRA, one avoids paying tax on a lump sum while keeping the growth and tax deferral of the IRA intact. But those days are over.

The SECURE Act was passed by Congress in December 2019. One of its provisions eliminated Stretch IRAs for those who inherited an IRA from January 1, 2020.

Now, truth be told, too many IRA beneficiaries took the money and ran (taking a lump sum) despite the very real attraction of stretching. That was probably shortsighted.

Anyway, the new law only allows for a maximum 10-year stretch for most non-spousal beneficiaries. Beneficiaries could take the lump sum or must completely empty the account by the end of the 10th year. The same new rules apply to tax-free ROTHs and all traditional IRAs, 401(k)s, etc.

Yes, these new laws apply to any IRS-qualified account, no matter where it was invested (stock/bond accounts, CDs, bank accounts, annuities, gold, etc.).

But what about non-qualified money (non-IRA-type funds)? Well, one could always set up a trust. But those can be costly to form and maintain. And you need a trustee, too. Why would someone consider a trust?

A trust can be a great solution for a beneficiary who should not receive a lump sum. Perhaps they are not good with money or are a gambler, an alcoholic, etc.

Many beneficiaries just aren't equipped to manage an inheritance, as it may be intentionally or unknowingly mishandled.

Of course, most of those folks would likely want to take the lump sum—but Mom and Dad know better. They don't want their legacy mishandled by an adult child who isn't prepared to handle their remaining life savings.

So is there another solution than a trust? Well, a few annuity contracts provide the owner with an optional way to "rule from the grave." To make sure their beneficiaries have no access to or limited access (based on the parent's wishes) to the lump sum death benefit.

The annuity owner(s), mom, and/or dad would decide if they wanted full or partial restrictions and to which child.

The proceeds of the annuity at death would be paid out monthly or quarterly over the beneficiary's lifetime or a ten or 20-year certain period—and as an FIA, they have zero market risk. The beneficiary's initial life expectancy factor is calculated using the IRS Single Life Table.

These non-qualified stretch annuities are not for everyone, but surely there are folks out there who don't even know there is a safe, no-cost, tax-deferred alternative to a trust.

Vanguard's Market Projections

Throughout this book, I've been referring to Vanguard's projections for the next decade. Well, here we are.

Take a look at what mutual fund giant Vanguard thinks is ahead for the markets over the next ten years on the next chart! It's nothing like the last ten years for sure.

Just take a peek at the next page. What do you think about Vanguard's latest projections for the next decade's various stock and bond markets? It's kind of depressing, isn't it?

To me, Vanguard seems to be making it pretty clear to diversify your portfolio with investments that cannot go down—without even saying so. Ones with a 0% floor so you can avoid market losses. And ones that lock in gains and can reset to take advantage of the market volatility.

By the way, the "Medium Volatility" column means that in any given year, the expected range of returns might be 17.2% (for U.S. equities) above or below the expected range of returns shown for each type of asset.

So, in any given year, U.S. equities might return between -12.8% to +21.6% (with only medium volatility, which means about two-thirds of the years). Of course, returns could be way worse than that as we saw in 2008 (-37%), 2022 (-18%), or, of course, way better, as in 2019 (+30%).

Vanguard is projecting that with all those likely gains and

losses, you should plan on your US equities to only average 4.4%-6.4% over that time period—including having years with big losses and big gains over the next decade.

Vanguard's outlook for financial markets

Our 10-year annualized nominal return and volatility forecasts are shown below. They are based on the December 31, 2022, running of the Vanguard Capital Markets Model® (VCMM). Equity returns reflect a 2-point range around the 50th percentile of the distribution of probable outcomes. Fixed income returns reflect a 1-point range around the 50th percentile. More extreme returns are possible.

EQUITIES	RETURN PROJECTION	MEDIAN VOLATILITY	FIXED INCOME	RETURN PROJECTION	MEDIAN VOLATILITY
U.S. equities	4.4%–6.4%	17.2%	U.S. aggregate bonds	4.0%–5.0%	5.5%
U.S. value	4.5%–6.5%	19.8%	U.S. Treasury bonds	3.6%–4.6%	5.8%
U.S. growth	2.4%–4.4%	18.3%	U.S. credit bonds	4.5%–5.5%	5.2%
U.S. large-cap	4.3%–6.3%	16.9%	U.S. high-yield corporate bonds	6.1%–7.1%	10.2%
U.S. small-cap	4.7%–6.7%	22.6%	U.S. Treasury Inflation-Protected Securities	3.0%–4.0%	5.0%
U.S. real estate investment trusts	4.6%–6.6%	20.3%	U.S. cash	3.4%–4.4%	1.4%
Global equities ex-U.S. (unhedged)	6.7%–8.7%	18.5%	Global bonds ex-U.S. (hedged)	3.9%–4.9%	4.4%
Global ex-U.S. developed markets equities (unhedged)	6.5%–8.5%	16.7%	Emerging markets sovereign bonds	5.6%–6.6%	10.6%
Emerging markets equities (unhedged)	6.3%–8.3%	26.3%	**U.S. inflation**	2.0%–3.0%	2.3%

Notes: These probabilistic return assumptions depend on current market conditions and, as such, may change over time.

IMPORTANT: The projections or other information generated by the Vanguard Capital Markets Model regarding the likelihood of various investment outcomes are hypothetical in nature, do not reflect actual investment results, and are not guarantees of future results. Distribution of return outcomes from the VCMM are derived from 10,000 simulations for each modeled asset class. Simulations are as of December 31, 2022. Results from the model may vary with each use and over time. For more information, see page 4.

Source: Vanguard Investment Strategy Group

Suppose the stock market only averages 5%-7% annually for the next ten years, as Vanguard (and others) predict. In that case, you might also need some different non-annuity strategies for the "at-risk" side of your portfolio.

Notice what Vanguard projects for bond returns over the next decade? All types of bond offerings range from 3%-4% for TIPS to 6%-7% for risky high-yield "junk" bonds. BUFFER annuities should do better than those projected returns of bonds plus the annual lock-in and reset. And guaranteed lifetime income is something bonds can't do.

Yet, despite current bond interest rates (and extremely low rates for the last 5 years) and projected returns going forward, look at how investor money is flowing into bond funds and ETFs. Truly buying high (and likely selling lower).

Again, our advisory firm has some proven ideas for other bond alternatives and less volatile stock strategies that you might want to hear more about. Given Vanguard's projections, does more diversification make sense? Why?

The Two Retirement Doors

If you are already retired or close to retiring, are you 100% sure that you are going to have a great retirement, or do you have some doubts? What about if one of you lives well into your nineties?

It's really pretty simple—whether you lean toward "probability-based" or "safety-first," there can only be one actual result.

You see, there are only two possible doors to go through at retirement. Door #1: is that your MONEY will outlive you. Door #2: is that YOU will outlive your money! There is NO 3rd door!

There are some 10,000 Americans who retire every day. Many of those folks are in deep trouble. Most do not have a written, date-specific retirement savings or an income distribution plan. No plan for longevity, inflation, market volatility, or rising taxes.

What I refer to as either an "income allocation" plan or a retirement roadmap.

Most of them fully realize it, but they don't know what to do to fix it. Sure, you want to walk through Door #1 but do you have a real plan to do so? No matter how long you might live? No matter what markets do to you?

Whether you are still saving for retirement or are currently retired, do you know exactly how much money it is going to take for you to retire comfortably when you want to... and/or for you and your spouse to REMAIN comfortably retired?

We've discussed sequence of returns risk throughout this book and the big difference between saving for accumulation and retirement income distribution.

How much market risk do you need to take to get the returns needed to afford the retirement lifestyle that you've been wanting for decades? How much drawdown can you emotionally handle? Do you know?

Well, a non-scientific answer, but one that most people close to or already in retirement can usually relate to, would be... "as LITTLE risk as necessary."

Here's another way to put this all-important retirement question. What potential return is worth "hoping" to get to put much of your life savings at risk? Is it for a 20% potential return? A 12%, 9%, or maybe 7% return?

We all understand the ratio of risk and reward. The more risk one takes, the higher the potential reward should be. But we know that higher risk means that not only might we get bigger potential returns, but we must also endure and live with a much greater chance of loss... and stress while taking withdrawals for our retirement lifestyle.

Where should you invest to get the highest potential returns with the lowest drawdowns possible? When is a "good time" to lose money?

Most folks need to take some risk in their income allocation plan to reach their retirement income goals. So, it's not "if" you take investment risks or not, but how much risk you need to take to reach your retirement income and legacy goals.

Do you remember the example of the two sisters, Jane and Jill, who retired just three years apart with the same $1,000,000 of assets? Jane's savings grew despite taking the same withdrawals as Jill. Jane was lucky indeed.

Jill simply retired three years too late and suffered from a bad sequence of returns. Jill was unlucky.

As far as stock market risk goes, does it make sense to be opportunistic in good times (enjoy the fruits of the market) and defensive in bad times? That's the goal of our portfolio strategies with daily oversight by our full-time investment committee for non-FIA investments.

A few pages back, I mentioned how people have fears, doubts, and uncertainties about their retirement planning. That's entirely natural, as paychecks from working cease. It seems to me that they are looking for peace of mind, stability, freedom, independence, simplicity, and any other intangible needs.

Well, here are some reasons that my clients told me why they wanted my professional planning help:

** "We're afraid we're not doing the right things with my money. There's too much conflicting information out there. Information overload!"
** "I just want to simplify my investments since it's too frustrating to keep up with them all."
** "I don't think you can ever have enough money."
** "We want to keep the same lifestyle in retirement as we had while we were working."
** "I definitely do not want to end up like my folks—old, watching every single dollar, and always worried."
** "I don't want to be weighed down with details."
** "I don't want to pay any more taxes than I have to."
** "This is the first time we've ever retired. We don't want to mess it up."
** "I want to make sure my family is taken care of— especially my wife, if I go first."
** "We don't want us to be a burden on our children."
** "What accounts should we withdraw from first?"
** "I want an advisor to help keep me on course and not let me be distracted by headlines and emotions."

Will You OUTLIVE Your MONEY? Check this out!
Find Out in 9 Quick Steps
www.smartfinancialplanning.com/FindOutHere

I always ask my clients what they want out of their money and their life (goals) and then help them stay on track and overcome the bumps we know will happen along the way. Bumps are just part of life.

Full disclosure—how do I get paid on all FIAs?

Essentially, it's the same way I get paid for managing portfolios at Fidelity or Schwab.

The insurance companies pay me 0.25% quarterly on your account balance (1% per year) to help you manage the annuity for as long as you keep the money in the account.

My 0.25% fee does NOT come out of/reduce your account balance. It does NOT lower your potential returns at all.

There are no sales loads (and often no fees unless you opt to buy more options for potentially higher returns). It is very much in our mutual interest to have your account grow (with or without any fees). I think you will want to keep going beyond the 7 or 10-year holding period. It's my job to make you very satisfied (and you can always take 7%-10% of your deposit out each year without penalty).

But suppose something better comes along in the future. In that case, we can always move the account to something that better suits any new goals or changing circumstances after the initial holding period.

As a fee-based Certified Financial Planner™, I act as a fiduciary whether I'm charging a fixed fee for a retirement income plan, managing assets at Fidelity or Schwab, or recommending life insurance or annuities.

The CLIENT (under the Fiduciary standard) is at the center of all planning—not the PRODUCT (Suitability standard). I must always put the client's interest first and recommend what I would do if I had the same financial goals and were in the same situation. It's good business practice, too.

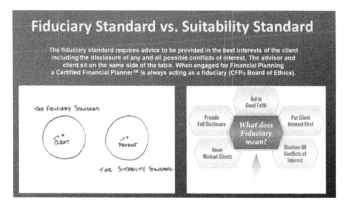

Again, the FIAs discussed in this book are not your ordinary fixed-indexed annuities sold by many agents for a big commission. You deserve better.

They are unique for either their "safe accumulation" purpose and for use in my market-savvy RMD or withdrawal strategy—or to provide more income than the "4% rule" with a lower initial investment.

And as a fiduciary, I'll let you know if any of these annuities make sense for your personal situation and circumstances. But for the right goals and circumstances, I believe they are diamonds in the rough.

I'll leave you with one more chart on the next page that I posted on LinkedIn a while back. It's titled: "Is Targeting Yield/Dividends a Risky Strategy?"

It shows the drawdown (peak to trough losses) in various asset classes. Look at the bond categories and see what their historical maximum drawdown has been. Negative -12%, -17%, -30%, and -35%. It is not typical, but it happens.

Bonds aren't quite as safe as many folks believe they are. And check out the drawdowns of the equities! Peak to trough losses in various equity classes of up to 65%.

From 01/11/1973 to 10/3/1974, the S&P 500 had a whopping drawdown of -48.2%. From 11/28/1980 to 8/12/1982, the drawdown was "only" -27.1%.

And from 8/25/1987 to 12/4/1987, the total drawdown was -33.5%.

More recently, from 3/24/2000 to 10/9/2002, the S&P 500 had a huge drawdown of -49.1%. From 10/9/2007 to 3/9/2009, the S&P 500 had a massive drawdown of -56.8%. And in the short-lived COVID crash of 2/19/2020 to 3/23/2020, there's a loss of -33.9% in the index.

Is Targeting Yield/Dividends a Risky Strategy?

So again, FIAs can never suffer market losses. No market-based drawdowns. ZERO is your HERO.

As in 2022, in a 60/40 portfolio, bond drawdowns can occur at the same time that equities are tanking. The smart RMD or income withdrawal strategy described in this book can help keep you from "selling low" and allow your investments to recover—as markets always have.

And the past "NET" returns (even after paying a fee for more upside) of 5%, 6%, or even higher aren't too shabby. I genuinely expect any of these annuities to outperform bonds. And they might even outperform stocks over the next decade if Vanguard's projections come true. The 0% floor and lock-in and reset mechanisms are the secret sauces that make them attractive (but not perfect).

If you have an interest in exploring any of these potential

options as a bond (or stock) alternative for a traditional IRA or ROTH, 401(k) rollover, or taxable brokerage account, please contact me for more information.

We would look at how these types of products may make sense for yourself or someone you care about, (such as a parent or sibling) as part of an accumulation strategy or a retirement withdrawal plan.

Of course, there will be no obligation, cost, or hassle. I've been a professional fee-based planner for over 20 years—not a starving insurance agent. There's no cost to you to investigate these or any of my financial services further.

I am licensed in most states for insurance and nearly every state as an Investment Advisor Representative with other non-traditional "bond-alternative" and equity strategies for investors who want higher returns with less risk. We also offer research-driven, non-cookie-cutter investment portfolios to limit drawdown in both equities and bonds.

I'm sure that your current advisor isn't talking about them.

I look forward to the opportunity to discuss how any of my professional services can improve your financial future by reducing your risks, taxes, and stress. Learn more about my smart strategies to grow, protect and manage your wealth, retirement income and legacy!

Simply send me an email or give my office a call to see if what I do for my clients is what you are looking for.

About the Author: Mark J. Orr, CFP® RICP®
PROACTIVE Tax Planning, LLC
www.SmartFinancialPlanning.com
770-777-8309 Office
mark@SmartFinancialPlanning.com

Mark has been a practicing Certified Financial Planner™ since 2000. Certified Financial Planners are held to the strictest ethical and fiduciary standards. He has also earned the year-long Retirement Income Certified Professional® (RICP®) designation. Since 1997, he has held life, health, and the Series 7 Securities license (no longer maintained) and became a Registered Investment Advisor soon after owning his own fee-based firm from 1999-2016.

He is now an Investment Advisor Representative with Retirement Wealth Advisors (RWA), where he manages his clients' stock and bond market-based investments—applying tactical money management mainly using index ETFs. These fee-only accounts are allocated into portfolios based on a client's risk tolerance, tax situation, time horizon, and income and legacy goals. Mark always acts in his role as a fiduciary.

He is a 4-time past board member of his Rotary Club and continues to be active in community service through the Rotary Club. On a personal note, Mark and Norma live in Alpharetta, Georgia, and love to travel—especially to warm sandy beaches. Staying in good shape is very important to him, and he enjoys excellent red wine.

Finally, he is the very proud father of three grown children (Megan, Marina, and Michael) and two wonderful grandchildren.

Acknowledgments and Disclosures

The opinions and views written in this book are those of the author and do not necessarily represent those of any person, organization, or firm that I have been associated with (either in the past, currently, or maybe in the future). This book is intended to provide general information only, and no individual professional financial advice is offered herein. The author is not a CPA or certified tax professional. The author is not an attorney. Neither the author nor publisher intend to or is rendering any professional services, including but not limited to tax advice, investment advice, insurance advice, legal advice, or mortgage advice. Neither this book nor any words written within its pages should be interpreted as giving any such personal/individual advice and should not be relied upon. Any mention of financial products, investment managers, investment advisory services, etc., should not be construed as an offer to buy, sell, or exchange any financial product or service.

The author and publisher disclaim any responsibility for any reader taking any liability or loss incurred as a consequence of any implementation (or even non-implementation) of the information provided herein.

No book intended as general information and sold to the general public can be construed to offer specific and personal financial, investment, insurance, tax, or legal advice. All readers who require personal advice and professional financial service should seek an experienced, qualified, and appropriately licensed advisor (relevant to such advice) and not solely rely on the contents of this or any other book to make any personal financial decision.

Insurance products are not investments. All insurance products are backed based solely on the financial strength and the claims-paying ability of the insurer that issues the policy or contract. Use of the terms "Principal Protected," "Guaranteed," "Safe," "Secure," and any and all such similar words when describing any insurance product are based entirely on the fact of contractual guarantees that rely on the financial strength and claims-paying ability of the insurance company.

Fixed Indexed Annuity (FIA) and IUL insurance policies are not stock, bond, or investments and have no direct participation in the stock or bond markets. You are not buying any bonds, shares of stocks, or shares in an index, nor do they include dividends or interest of any stock, bond, or market index.

Investment Advisory Services are offered through Retirement Wealth Advisors (RWA), an SEC Registered Investment Advisor. Mark J. Orr and RWA are not affiliated. Investing involves risk, including the potential loss of principal. No investment strategy can guarantee a profit or protect against loss in periods of declining values. Opinions expressed are subject to change without notice and are not intended as investment advice or to predict future performance.

Past performance does not guarantee future results. Consult your financial professional before making any investment decision. All life insurance, fixed annuity products, fees for retirement income plans and advanced income tax planning for business owners are sold separately through Mark J. Orr, CFP®, and/or PROACTIVE Tax Planning LLC.

You Might Be Interested to Read the Book Descriptions of Just 3 of My Other Books on the Pages That Follow.
All are available in paperback or KINDLE on Amazon.com

—Get Me to ZERO—

Whose retirement are you planning for—YOURS... OR Uncle Sam's?

It's your choice. I'm planning to pay as little as ZERO income taxes in my retirement. How about you?

Get Me to ZERO™ describes seven synergistic tax strategies to help you legally get your future assets and cash flow off the IRS's radar screen and pay as little as ZERO income taxes during retirement.

My book explains how implementing these seven proven tax strategies can offer up to 20%-40% more spendable retirement income than traditional 401(k)s and IRAs.

Of course, ROTH contributions and conversions are fully discussed. Those are 2 of the 7 strategies. Also described are two amazing, little-known, tax-free strategies using OPM (Other People's Money).

I've been a practicing Certified Financial Planner™ (CFP®) for over 20 years, serving clients across the country. Most of them I've never met.

My financial planning practice and this book are centered on these firm beliefs:
1) People should not pay a dime more in taxes than the law requires

2) Nor should they take an ounce more risk than necessary to reach their financial goals.

Judge Learned Hand, a federal district and appellate judge for more than 50 years, is said to have been the most influential judge in the U.S. who never sat on the Supreme Court.

Judge Hand said, "**Anyone may arrange his affairs so that his taxes shall be as low as possible;** he is not bound to choose that pattern which best pays the treasury. There is not even a patriotic duty to increase one's taxes."

"Over and over again, the Courts have said that **there is nothing sinister in so arranging affairs to keep taxes as low as possible**. Everyone does it, rich and poor alike, for nobody owes any public duty to pay more than the law demands."

That, in a nutshell, is the legal basis for the Get Me to ZERO™ strategies. Proactively and systematically arranging our financial affairs so that our future income taxes will be as low as possible.

And this book is not about tax loopholes! Not one strategy is a loophole.

Author Tom Wheelwright (he's Rich Dad Poor Dad's personal CPA) says, **"After all, the tax law is really a map— a treasure map. As you follow this map, your taxes go down."**

The more sources of non-taxable retirement cash flow—the better. Use the full tax code to make as much of your retirement cash flow legally "invisible" to the IRS. There are not even lines for these tax-free incomes on your 1040 tax form. None.

If we can't eliminate future income taxes in retirement, we at least want to minimize them by becoming fully informed. Proactively using the tax code as it is written and intended is legal tax avoidance—NOT tax evasion.

Does your current retirement planning include planning for future income taxes? Do you have a tax-smart exit strategy for your 401(k) and IRA so that you can spend and enjoy more of your hard-earned savings—and pay the IRS less?

The primary goal of this book is to show people how to implement a holistic and comprehensive planning approach that employs several tax-diverse strategies to help people become more financially confident and secure today while preparing for an extraordinary retirement.

Be tax savvy. Pay the IRS less. Keep more and have a better life!

On to the next book description...

—*Retirement Income Planning*—

In planning for retirement, "Income… is the outcome that matters."

"Income… is the <u>outcome</u> that matters."

Tony Robbins, world-famous speaker, motivator, and author of the best-selling book "MONEY Master the Game," wrote that epic sentence. Among other topics, his book stresses the importance of "setting up a lifetime income plan."

Tony is 100% correct, but 75% of retirees do not have a retirement plan at all. Not even a bad plan.

"If you fail to plan, you are planning to fail!"—Benjamin Franklin

Is your current plan to wing it? See how it goes? Hope for the best?

There are only two possible doors to go through at retirement.
Door #1 is that your MONEY will outlive you.
Door #2 is that YOU will outlive your money.
There is NO 3rd door!

My book describes how to form a 30-plus-year monthly cash-flow retirement plan based not on speculation, hopes, or dreams but on as much certainty and predictability as possible.

I have been a practicing Certified Financial Planner for more than 20 years. I've been building hundreds of easy-to-understand, written retirement income plans for clients across the U.S.A. It is that long and varied professional experience that formed the seeds of my 2nd book.

This book is written for people within ten years of retirement OR who are already retired and looking for a better "plan."

With lots of educational retirement planning information spread throughout the book, it culminates into 3 example client lifetime income plans that show how combining Social Security, any pensions, investments, and insurance can help you enjoy an increasing lifelong income while reducing the top 5 retirement risks. What are those risks?

Those top 5 retirement risks that too few people are actually planning for are: inflation, stock and bond market risks, rising health care costs, the likelihood of higher taxes, and the granddaddy of them all—living too long.

It's really all about creating a dependable and increasing lifetime monthly cash flow that gives one true financial freedom and peace of mind—during what could likely be a 30-plus-year retirement.

Rather than "Asset Allocation," that most planners talk about, I devote the bulk of my practice (and writing) to "Income Allocation" and "Strategy Allocation."

These can dramatically reduce the top 5 risks people will face in retirement. Again, it comes down to: "Income… is the <u>outcome</u> that matters." For most Americans, it's the ONLY outcome that matters.

My —**Retirement Income Planning**— book explains many smart and safe retirement planning strategies and ideas to accomplish that. It covers the bases that you need to know to help avoid making a planning mistake and help make sure that you go through Door #1.

Many books on this subject are written by writers, not actual practicing financial planners who are taking care of real people with real money and their retirement dreams.

Get educated on the "real world" of retirement income planning from a planner in the trenches every day.

"If you fail to plan, you are planning to fail!"

Will You OUTLIVE Your MONEY? Check this out!
Find Out in 9 Quick Steps
www.smartfinancialplanning.com/FindOutHere

On to the last book description…

—Social Security Income Planning: The 2024 Baby Boomers Guide—

On November 4, 2015, this book was cited, and I was quoted in a USA Today article about the new Social Security rules:

"The decision on how and when to file for Social Security should be made as part of an overall retirement income plan with your financial goals, life expectancies, and financial fears firmly in mind."

It's your money. You paid $100,000s into the system your whole life (FICA taxes)—so don't leave $10,000s of benefits sitting on the table that cannot be retrieved.

It's my goal for both the middle-class and affluent Baby Boomers to realize that this is an important decision.

Using the "4% rule," a $2,000 monthly Social Security check is worth some $600,000. How much thought should you give to an "investment" of that size?

Too many people have no idea of what their real benefit options are—and, unfortunately, can be prone to miss out on all the money they qualify for. Several useful examples are given to show you the full range of filing options and how to maximize the lifetime benefits you deserve. Written by an experienced Certified Financial Planner, this book is for soon-to-be retirees who want to learn about the different claiming strategies and ramifications of each (whether you are married, never married, divorced, or widowed).

As you are reading the book, it becomes very apparent that I actually work in the retirement income planning field daily with real people's savings, their Social Security filing options—and their retirement dreams.

But let me be clear that there is NOTHING about Social Security DISABILITY income payments or Supplemental Security Income (SSI) in my book (which caused some early negative reviews). If that's what you are looking for, don't buy this book.

My book's sole purpose is to provide people who are about to retire with all the information that they need to make the best Social Security benefit decisions based on their unique financial circumstances and retirement goals. In this respect, it is an essential planning guide.

Perhaps one of the most unique portions of the book is where I combine my expertise in Social Security with my knowledge of income taxes to show readers how it is very possible to cut one's taxable income and subsequent retirement income tax bill by 50%.

The example comparing the Earlys, the Waites, and the Bests show what's possible.

That alone is worth multiple times the book's price, as it explains how a savvy reader can save $1,000s of income tax dollars each year during their retirement by fully understanding how Social Security is taxed.

The chapter about the 3 buckets of investment risk and the 3 taxation buckets is the perfect complement to learning about filing strategies since Social Security was never meant to provide for all of one's retirement income.

—**Social Security Income Planning**—is concise and written in a conversational style, yet it's jam-packed with non-stop tips, warnings, things to consider, and much more you need to maximize your benefits.

Again, the book rightfully stresses how your decision to file for your Social Security benefits should not be made on a "standalone basis." Your claiming decisions should be made in conjunction with your overall retirement income goals, your assets and other income resources, your adversity to risk, your (and your spouse's) likely longevity, etc. This book helps put all those factors into perspective.

It is a big decision. Don't let ignorance cause you to make a filing mistake that could cost you a higher guaranteed lifetime income. Get Smart!

Made in the USA
Las Vegas, NV
16 February 2024

85858185R00079